IN THE TRACKS OF THE
'CORNISH RIVIERA E

Amyas Crump

NOODLE BOOKS

ISBN 978 1 909328 22 8 Printed in England by
Berforts Information Press

First published in 2014 by Kevin Robertson under the
NOODLE BOOKS imprint

PO Box 279, Corhampton, SOUTHAMPTON. SO32 3ZX

www.noodlebooks.co.uk

Front cover - Truro shed closed to steam in March 1962 and completely in November 1965. West Signal Box following on 7 November 1971, desolation abounds as sleepers are cleared prior to building of new industrial units.

Previous page - Not only did the *Cornish Riviera Express* run in several parts for much of its life, the places served were also catered for by a range of other connecting and through services. Very much 'In the tracks of the *Cornish Riviera Express*' is this shot of an immaculate single chimney 6023 *King Edward 11* passing gangers at Dawlish Warren c1957 complete with *Cornish Riviera Limited* headboard and a full rake of brown and cream Mk1 stock. Hopefully, 6023 will be able to visit this location again before too long, having been restored to working order at Didcot Railway Centre

Right - Ready to leave Paddington is an immaculate green liveried Warship displaying headcode 1A30 the *Cornish Riviera* itself. In the background is one of the Blue Pullman sets, newly introduced in September 1960. The loco is thought to be either D823 *Hermes* or D825 *Intrepid*, both were only a few weeks old at this time.

Rear Cover - Age old rivalries between Devon and Cornwall over the origins of pasties and how to make a cream tea are forgotten by all in their appreciation of 'the bridge', spot-lit for its centenary in the summer of 1959.

Contents: based on the GWR Publication: 'Through the Window'

Introduction

With little previous experience of rail travel, other than seeing off the last passenger train from Hemyock, it came as something of a revelation to arrive at Paddington in the mid 1960s. The approach, I recall, was marked by several diesel shunters with their eye-catching and newly painted 'wasp stripes'. As we drew in to the platform, away to the left was a very grimy steam loco waiting to depart - probably a once grand 'Castle'. On the actual platform it was astonishing to see cars and taxi's drawn up beside us, and as for the number of luggage barrows, it was hard to believe that so many could exist. At that time, when Health & Safety was largely governed by common sense and a desire for self-preservation, we were able to enjoy Taxi's without a side door along with the open platform RT and RM (Routemaster) buses. Like the sun shinning on the immaculate maroon 'Western' and its matching train on the way home, these things proved more memorable than the tour of London Zoo which had been the true purpose of this lengthy excursion from the West country.

To a child, the journey itself was almost as interminable as the drive to St Ives where we took several summer holidays, there I recall something of the station - backing on to the beach, but like George Behrend in *Gone With Regret* it was to be many years before I completed the journey west by train.

Whilst the GWR *Through the window* guide may nowadays appear a little dated, the journey still has many spectacular moments; the daring of Maidenhead bridge, the ancient history of the white horses, whilst mist shrouded mysteries of the Somerset levels contrast with the first views of the sea approaching Dawlish. Then west of Newton are the lofty viaducts of which St Pinnock is the highest at 151 feet while from Truro Viaduct is the lovely view over the city and its waterfront. Finally Mounts Bay heralds journeys end at the rather modest terminus of Penzance. In the heyday of the Great Western the formation of *The Limited* included slip coaches and portions for; Weymouth, Minehead, Ilfracombe, Kingswear, Kingsbridge, Newquay, Falmouth and St Ives. In the 21st century it is interesting to note that First Great Western have recently revived a number of named services from yesteryear, including the *Cornish Riviera Express*. It is hoped that they will do justice to such an illustrious name, now approaching its 110th anniversary.

Left - Youthful admirers for the Fireman's handy-work, amidst the glow from the firebox door, as pannier 1504 sits at Paddington in-between carriage shunting duties.

Right - Looking towards the lawn and exit at Paddington, (far left). The absence of many passengers in this set suggests that perhaps they were taken on a Sunday morning, in which case, the Staff Band is likely to be playing on The Lawn - oh for that picture too!

Far right - The view back towards the vehicle entrance ramp, and with over thirty barrows in shot! All taken in May 1963.

Top Right - D1066 *Western Prefect* stands beside a similar number of tail lamps! It is unlikely that the Refreshments kiosk would have had any burgers on offer in 1969.

Dedicated to the memory of George Behrend whose book *Gone With Regret (Jersey Artists 1966)* explained to all of us who did not know the GWR, what we had missed and why it was so special.

There is nothing quite like a comfortable carriage seat to enjoy the view from, like an old friend, always there for us. But whose true value was not appreciated until they had gone. Now wherever we go in once familiar places, there are ghosts of the past. I hope this simple reminder brings back some happy memories of what was for many years, the world's longest non-stop train service.

Amyas Crump Exeter 2014

For their patience, interest, help with research and photographs my grateful thanks are due to; Colin and Helen Billington, Colin Burges, Martin Boddy, Robin Fell, Duncan Ferguson, Paul Garnsworthy, Peter Gray, Great Western Trust, Brian Harding, Chris Henley, John Hill, Rod Holcombe, Stewart Hookins, Hugh Howes, Ian Langhorn, Peter Lugg, Bob LeMarchant, Colin Maggs, John Mann, David Massey, David Mitchell, Peter Mitchelmore, Gerry Nichols, Mrs S Nuell (Bristol City Library), Graham Parnell, Kevin Robertson, Martin Robinson, the late T W E Roche, Alan Sainty, Liz Shepherd, Geof Sheppard, Andrew Snowdon, Ian Stoyle, Martin Street, Chris Tilley, Tiverton Museum of Mid Devon Life, Andrew Toosey, Peter Triggs, Jon Trott, Mrs Margaret Warburton for permission to use images taken by the late Mark Warburton, Rosie Majer & Tim Maddocks of Network Rail and my family. Where known, photographers are credited, all others are from the authors own collection.

Left - For many, London is a place of travel, and iconic landmarks. Combining both is RT KXW113 on route 12 for Oxford Circus captured while passing what is now the Queen Elizabeth 11 tower with its well known clock faces. A little to the west of the hustle and bustle of central London is Paddington Station where in Great Western times, and well into BR days, 10.30am was departure time for those heading west on the *Cornish Riviera Express.*

Lower left + right - While businessmen, travellers and holidaymakers made their way to Paddington, there would be much activity to get the engine and train prepared - at Old Oak Common - and the empty stock moved, generally by one of the many pannier tanks allocated there, in to the platform. Standing in the shadows of the shed, next to one of its four turntables is 'Hall' Class 5989 *Cransley Hall* and more appropriate express motive power in the form of 'Castle' class 5070 *Sir Daniel Gooch.* The view was taken in July 1963. Another 50xx series Castle is hiding off to the left, with a painted cabside number, its days numbered. To the right, a shiny new bicycle heralds change with a brand new 'Western' just sneaking in to view. Enlargement suggests that this is D1065 *Western Consort,* allocated here from new only a few weeks previously. The empty stock working is in the hands of Hawkesworth pannier 9405, seen passing Scrubs Lane in October 1963.

Right - London's first major railway hotel opened in 1854 and gained Royal patronage shortly after with a formal visit by the Prince Consort and Prince of Wales (later King Edward V111). Other than the original façade, most of the building now dates from the 1920s when it was completely rebuilt while remaining in everyday use. This luggage label dates from the late 1930s, the roundel motif being the first railway corporate logo.

Below far right - The GWR Publicity Department produced one of their well known books for boys of all ages, in 1923 and by February 1924 seventy-one thousand copies of "The 10.30 Limited" had been printed! Within its description of Paddington, the reader learns that the War Memorial was erected in honour of the 25,479 GW men who served in the Great War, of whom 2,524 gave their lives. These numbers had considerably increased by WW2, at the end of which 3,312 men and women of the staff had given their lives. Most major stations had a framed Roll of Honour .

Bottom left + centre -The memorial is to be found on Platform one under the balcony, from which in days gone by the General Manager and Directors enjoyed a view across what came to be known as 'Brunel's Cathedral'

A timely trip to London resulted in this extraordinary view of the process by which the well known landmark of Bishops Road bridge was replaced. As can be seen, the old span was raised, the replacement gradually jacked out across the lines, and when complete the original was lowered back down on to the replacement and broken up for scrap. 3 February 2005. (Courtesy J Trott)

In line with the 'Through the Window' guides of days gone by, a map of the routes covered, is included throughout this volume. Very few of these stations were served by *'The Limited'* as it is known, but all would have been seen from the passing train.

ROUTE MAPS

⬤ OPEN STATIONS..IVER
◯ CLOSED STATIONS...BRENT
SLIP COACH ROUTES + THROUGH COACHES........*NEWQUAY*
(COURTESY 'ATLAS OF THE GREAT WESTERN RAILWAY' R A COOKE)

Right - Stock has arrived and suitable motive power backs down from Old Oak Common: coupling up watched over by the Fireman who will later be shovelling most of that four-ton pile of coal from the tender to the firebox. Each shovel-full will need to be carefully placed to get the best out of the engine. For steam crews, the next stop would be Plymouth.

During the Indian summer of steam in the late 1950s, one of Churchward's powerful 47xx loco's could often be found on summer Saturday trains to the west. In this case it is 4704 that is looking beautifully turned out. Much of the fine work of this small class of engines was on long distance, fast freights, running at night. All have long since gone, but were not forgotten. With the originals being unnamed, the project to build a new 4709 based on recycling many standard parts from other scrap engines, has taken on the marketing name of *Night Owl* - a reflection of when most of their work was done, but not a name they were known by during their working lives.

PADDINGTON
GATEWAY TO THE WEST

Left - Not all engines went to Old Oak Common for servicing. Although it was only three miles away, traffic demands were frequently such that engines were turned and serviced at the tiny Ranelagh Bridge engine sidings, only a short distance out of Paddington on the down side. Long after the demise of steam, the yard is still in use and has all its steam facilities extant, along with some suitably period rolling stock in the form of an ex SR PMV and a slightly younger tank wagon. English Electric built 50 036 *Victorious* in large logo livery runs past the old yard on its way in to Paddington. The site is now used for car parking. I Langhorn, coll A Crump

PADDINGTON ● WESTBOURNE PARK ● ACTON ● BROADWAY EALING ● WEST EALING ● SOUTHALL ●

Kensal Green Cemetery on the Harrow Road is only a short distance away from the Great Western main line just before passing Old Oak Common. It therefore seems a most appropriate place to find, almost hidden under a tree, the Brunel family tomb. In this tranquil corner lie the graves of several generations of this family so closely connected to the railway. September 2005. Courtesy J Trott

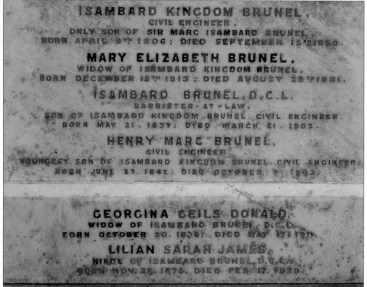

ISAMBARD KINGDOM BRUNEL,
CIVIL ENGINEER,
ONLY SON OF SIR MARC ISAMBARD BRUNEL,
BORN APRIL 9TH 1806: DIED SEPTEMBER 15TH 1859.
MARY ELIZABETH BRUNEL,
WIDOW OF ISAMBARD KINGDOM BRUNEL,
BORN DECEMBER 18TH 1813: DIED AUGUST 25TH 1881.
ISAMBARD BRUNEL, D.C.L.
BARRISTER-AT-LAW,
SON OF ISAMBARD KINGDOM BRUNEL, CIVIL ENGINEER,
BORN MAY 21, 1837: DIED MARCH 21, 1902.
HENRY MARC BRUNEL,
CIVIL ENGINEER,
YOUNGEST SON OF ISAMBARD KINGDOM BRUNEL, CIVIL ENGINEER,
BORN JUNE 27, 1842: DIED OCTOBER 7, 1903.

GEORGINA GEILS DONALD,
WIDOW OF ISAMBARD BRUNEL, D.C.L.
BORN OCTOBER 30, 1836: DIED MAY 17, 1911.
LILIAN SARAH JAMES,
NIECE OF ISAMBARD BRUNEL, D.C.L.
BORN NOV. 26, 1875, DIED FEB. 17, 1929.

OLD OAK COMMON

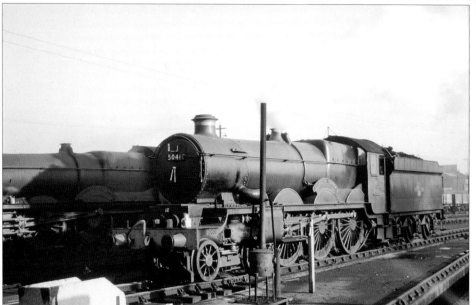

Left - Passing Old Oak Common, there would be plenty of activity whatever the hour. With the tender piled high and the safety valve just lifting, 5041 *Tiverton Castle* - an appropriate name for a journey west - is about ready to go. In front is a fire devil and its supply bunker, and to the right is the hitching post for an apparently absent water column. No 5041 is immaculate, but behind Modified Hall 6965 *Thirlestaine Hall* looks much less respectable although she still has another eight years to go and was destined to outlive 5041. D Borthwick coll A Crump
Opposite bottom left - While Maidenhead bridge was built, there was a temporary terminus beside the A4, east of the town. An entrance can still be found behind the vegetation on the Down side.

Southall was for many years the headquarters of the Great Western Road Motor Department, with an ever growing fleet of omnibuses and delivery vehicles. Guy FBB YF714 entered service in March 1927 at Penzance being withdrawn only four years later. After spending over forty years next to the sea near Newquay, and having suffered several alterations, it was sold for restoration. Another twenty five years of little progress followed before transfer to the Thames Valley & Great Western Omnibus Trust. After considerable research, work started on 1 January 2000. The results are seen here on 30 June 2013, No 1268 on some of the old GWR routes around Slough: here at Farnham Royal and Maidenhead. The vehicle had a further outing on 17 August 2013 to re-enact the 110th anniversary of the inauguration of GWR services from Helston to The Lizard.

MAIDENHEAD
JUNCTION FOR THE WYCOMBE LINE

Maidenhead East Yard finds 7808 *Cookham Manor* on an up parcels working - note the leading Hawkesworth full brake with its regular working painted on the side. In the down loop is 92236 on a freight, a busy scene that has already seen much change. For the future forthcoming electrification will bring with it a new vista of overhead wires. 7 May 1960. G T Robinson coll A Crump

HAYES & HARLINGTON

WEST DRAYTON & YIEWSLEY

IVER

LANGLEY (BUCKS)

SLOUGH

BURNHAM (BUCKS)

A cold January morning with the sun out, produces ideal conditions for the photographer waiting near a boarded up Waltham Siding Signal Box between Maidenhead and Twyford. Old Oak Common allocated Castle class 4096 *Highclere Castle* heads a westbound parcels, while Southall's 1474 heads towards Maidenhead, perhaps she has been away on loan? 26th January 1962. Nearby White Waltham Airfield was the wartime base for the Air Transport Auxiliary, whose many women pilots included Amy Johnson. One incident which must have been particularly disconcerting at this lonely outpost, came in July 1944 when a Halifax bomber with a live bomb load crash-landed not far away on the railway! G T Robinson coll A Crump

Right –The home of 'Railway Assortment Biscuits', with a system of sidings operated by fireless loco's, at Messrs Huntley & Palmers of Reading, July 1968.

Below –The town also had an extensive trolleybus network VRD186 demonstrates the Wokingham Road turning circle. 24 September 1968

A different form of electric traction was available at Reading (Southern), but on this occasion steam reigns supreme as N class 31862 of 75B Redhill shed, waits at Reading South while the peak-capped Station Master converses with the crew at the sane time keeping an eye on his watch. Above the tender is the clock tower of the Western station (seen again on the next page), where it can be noted that the chimneys of this listed building have been removed and capped. A prominent landmark in the town for over one hundred and fifty years, recent redevelopment of the station has dwarfed it completely. Control of the Southern station was transferred to the Western Region in March 1965, with closure following in September when services were moved to the new platform 4A, to be built on 'the bank' but occupied here by a temporary car park. The same area was also used by locospotters and Thames Valley buses.

Right - Centre right, the Station Garage (centre right) is the frontage of where the old SER station buildings once stood, beyond which cars are parked on what had been the space occupied by the platforms. The new platform 4A is to the right of a class 50 bringing in a train from Paddington. In the distance the prominent new office block reflects a sense of change in the character of the town - this view taken from the railway's own skyscraper Western Tower, but which in 2013 is now defunct, a definite eyesore daubed as it is in graffiti. More recently Reading station looks more like the set from a science fiction movie, stainless steel and glass having replaced masonry and brickwork. In the distance the whole of the Up side of the station has lost its various yards and sidings, including that at Kings Meadow but which was still in use here c1980. On a positive note, as part of the recent redevelopment, the rail underpass to the ex SR lines has been reinstated.

Below - redevelopment of the ex SR station site is well underway in this October 1986 view.
T Harden coll A Crump

READING GENERAL

With the amalgamation of Southern services into Reading General, the third rail has got even closer to Brunel's station, although the buildings still look much as it they had for many decades. Looking at the current, rebuilt version, there is little to connect it with this view. On the far side, 50 036 *Repulse* stands next to an HST, photographed in March 1984.

T Harden coll A Crump

During the later days of steam, Bulleid Pacific's regularly worked through Reading West, to Oxford. Merchant Navy 35002 *Union Castle* about to cross the Oxford Road bridge and pass Oxford Road Junction Signal Box. Beyond the engine was the WR steam shed - later the diesel depot. The depot site has now been cleared to make way for a flyover allowing trains from the Midlands heading south an uninterrupted path across the London to Bristol main line.

READING WEST

Continuing west from Southcote Junction, commuters are still well served along this end of the Berks & Hants line, even though many of the buildings and much infrastructure has gone. Many will enthuse over a D1000 'Western' class diesel hydraulic, even in blue livery, but this incarnation of the *Cornish Riviera Express* (headcode 1B45) has little of the presence of its steam predecessor once hauled by an immaculate 'King' with chocolate and cream stock. Since this view was taken, the old shelter on the Down platform has gone, to be replaced by a bus-stop type shelter. All this is due to go soon, as electrification works progress. Just beyond Theale, busy stone and oil terminals have contributed much to the importance of the Berks & Hants as a freight route. Aldermaston had been the WW2 temporary location for the GWR head office staff, later Padworth Sidings on the South side of the line, saw vast tonnages of coal traffic much of which went to the nearby MoD establishment before all this was lost to road haulage.

THEALE

British Rail (W)

BR 4465/2

FIRST CLASS   № 003775

SPECIAL RACEGOERS EXCURSION TRAIN

From London (Paddington)
To NEWBURY Racecourse

DATE   2 9

NEWBURY RACECOURSE

To the end of their reign, 'King' class locomotives - always immaculate - were the preferred motive power for the Race Specials from Paddington to Newbury Racecourse - smartest of all being the Members Special. On some of the last return workings to Paddington are 6025 *King Henry 111* with the 4.05pm departure, and on the right, the famous bell gives away 6000 *King George V* in charge of the 4.10pm working, 24 November 1962. (The 'Z' prefix indicates a special working.)

Newbury Racecourse was followed quickly by East Junction, where the line from Didcot came in. Having climbed the Berkshire Downs, an equal amount of skill was necessary to bring unfitted freights safely down this side and safely on to the main line. Passing through Newbury, branch trains would turn towards Winchester and Southampton at Enborne Junction a mile further on. As always, rail distances have to be measured from a zero point, these are rarely seen marked, but here opposite the site of Newbury goods is the zero milepost for the Didcot, Newbury & Southampton Railway still in situ many years after closure of the line. (**Right**)

ALDERMASTON — MIDGHAM — THATCHAM — NEWBURY RACECOURSE — NEWBURY — KINTBURY

Right - An unexpected visitor to the Newbury Up bay normally frequented by branch trains to Didcot and local stoppers, L1 31786 has her oil pots topped up before joining the return leg of the 'Solent Limited' railtour to Waterloo on 30 April 1961.

Below - Newbury has long been a place of importance, the spacious site now providing much car parking, rather than being used for the Lambourn bay which was at the foot of the grassy bank. Gone too is the oak panelling and stained glass windows of the Refreshment Rooms alongside the bookstall on platform two. Ongoing electrification work from here to Reading and Paddington has necessitated rebuilding of many overbridges to increase clearance. In the centre cess, lengths of broad gauge era bridge rail still survived in 1977. P. Triggs coll A Crump

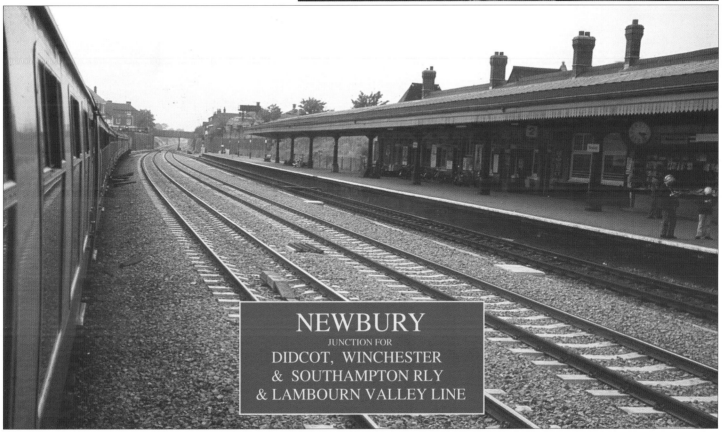

NEWBURY
JUNCTION FOR
DIDCOT, WINCHESTER
& SOUTHAMPTON RLY
& LAMBOURN VALLEY LINE

Left -As mentioned previously, the line to Winchester and Southampton diverged at Enborne Junction shortly before passing under this overbridge. Agriculture has largely obliterated the trackbed, although this bridge – still visible from passing trains, remains as a landmark. The railway has been following closely the Kennet & Avon Canal since Theale and from here on to Wootton Rivers, they remain side by side before the canal heads away towards Devizes, where it picks up another railway, that from Patney & Chirton to Holt Junction, route of the infamously slow Paddington - Bristol stopper (which ran on via Bradford on Avon and Bath). With over twenty locks on the canal between Newbury and the summit at Savernake so indicating a steady climb, the Fireman would be shovelling steadily from now on.

Below - After a long climb, it will soon be time for a breather as 4917 *Crosswood Hall* of Westbury, rounds the curve at Crofton in the afternoon sun of 8 August 1959. To the left is the canal pumping station. **Right** - With a bleaker backdrop, 59001 passes the same spot on 17 March 1999 on empties for Whatley Quarry. A. Morris + J Chalcraft both coll A. Crump

Just behind where the photographers had stood for the previous two shots, a connection from the east was made to the Midland & South Western Junction line to the south (hidden by the trees), with a further chord from the MSWJ to the westbound Berks & Hants. Between these two chords, the MSWJ had crossed over the mainline here near to Wolfhall Junction. The westbound 12.10 Paddington - Paignton was being hauled by D831 *Monarch* on 21 August 1971. J Crowley coll A Crump

HUNGERFORD ●   BEDWYN ●   SAVERNAKE (LOW LEVEL) ○   WOOTTON RIVERS HALT ○   PEWSEY ●   MANNINGFORD HALT ○

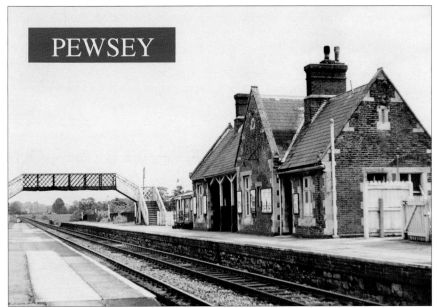

PEWSEY

Left - Now an award winning station, this was workaday Pewsey in 1969 by which time the building was already over a century old, having opened in 1862 when platform heights were rather lower. Shortly after this was taken, the footbridge was replaced by a secondhand one from Cookham (between Maidenhead and Bourne End). On the Up (left-hand) platform, a nineteenth century wooden waiting shelter was replaced in 1984, by a brick building sympathetically designed to match the station. The solid looking chimney stacks have also gone. Traffic is busy here, a wide rural catchment area which includes Marlborough - once having had two stations of its own. N Pratt coll A. Crump

Right - Looking North from Woodborough, some four miles away on Milk Hill, this White Horse is a prominent landmark. One of several in the area, this is perhaps the youngest, dating from 1812. It is 165 feet long, and like all the others would have taken considerable effort to cut away the turf from the white chalk downs.

Right - On 2 May 1965 No 6963 *Throwley Hall* paused at Patney & Chirton with the SLS *Wessex Downsman* railtour which it worked from Reading to Bristol Temple Meads, via Devizes. Evidently most photographers knew to keep off the track, but made full use of available vantage points! To the left is the 'old road' to Devizes, which has just had its track renewed, a sure sign of planned closure - which came the following April. A Hymek diesel heads east on the Westbury cut-off of 1906. In the background a footpath crosses the line via the footbridge, a useful marker for this location where the embankment of the Devizes line still gradually climbs away, but parallel for a mile or so before the two routes head west but curve away from each other.

After the opening of the direct route to Taunton - rather than via Bristol, the line through Devizes, and Holt Junction to Westbury remained a useful diversion route such as when a problematic landslip occurred at Crookwood in the summer of 1961. There were also the local and rather tedious long distance stopping services, including this one, the 2.35pm Paddington - Weston Super Mare in the charge of Castle 5071 *Hurricane* and looking rather hemmed in by the single line at Stert in July 1961.
P Strong coll A Crump

Slip working

Inset -Approaching Heywood Road Junction is a good point to include reference to the working of slip coaches. The lead compartment, fitted with end windows, was occupied by the Slip Guard who had a lever to operate at the appropriate moment. This opened up the drawbar hook, which, with self sealing valves on the steam heat and brake pipes allowed separation from the main train without affecting the emergency brake. The Slip Guard also had a gong and some braking power. A separate subsidiary signal lower down the post on the approach to the junction was provided for the slip, as this went in to the station for attaching to a Weymouth service, while the main train continued along the avoiding line.

WESTBURY

Right -The damp and decay of Westbury shed was still very much a carryover from the steam era in his atmospheric view of July 1971.

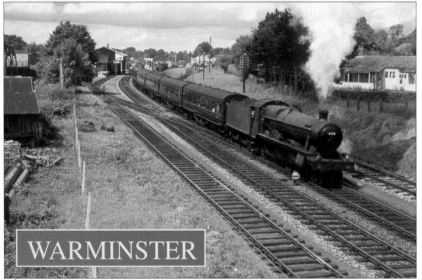

WARMINSTER

Above left + right - Changing times at Westbury, a steam railtour leaves past the Western Fuels coal depot: soon Yeoman stone traffic would justify removal of the coal yard to a road only industrial estate near Hawkeridge and instead the use of most available space at Westbury in connection with the stone haulage from the Mendips. The class 52 Western hauled train of PGA hoppers was passing through in April 1976.

Left - Westbury is a cross roads between the west of England line, north to Trowbridge and Bradford Junction, and south via Warminster to Salisbury. No 6988 *Swithland Hall* heads the 7.35am Nottingham to Bournemouth West service on 13 July 1963 at which time the permanent way was still kept in immaculate condition. Inter regional boundary changes of the early 1950s have brought this section into the Southern Region whose influence included the paint colour of the footbridge and upper quadrant signal by the goods shed.

WOODBOROUGH — PATNEY & CHIRTON — LAVINGTON — EDINGTON & BRATTON — WESTBURY WEYMOUTH SLIP — FROME

Although never adopted by the Southern, most other major lines made use of water troughs to enable long distance non stop running, the Great Western installing their first at Goring as far back as October 1895. From Paddington to the west, troughs were installed at Aldermaston, here at Fairwood, Creech and Exminster, all opening in June 1904. Troughs though were not necessarily placed at equal distances along the line, an important factor for any boiler was water quality, although water softening was also resorted to. From Paddington to Aldermaston was 45 miles with troughs of 560 yards, Fairwood 111 miles Down side trough was 553 yards and Up side 495 yards, Creech 159 miles 560 yards, and Exminster 200 miles with troughs of 560 yards. Reputedly another was installed a little later at Lostwithiel, but this would be a difficult location given the gradients and if used did not last long. To keep each trough topped up, a header tank of 18,750 gallons capacity was built at the midway point as here, intended to give a trough water level of five inches. A white lineside board - illuminated at night - would mark the start of the trough. With the end of steam working, the need for troughs disappeared but a short length survives on display at Didcot Railway Centre. In October 1957 an intrepid, but sadly unknown photographer has captured King class 6008 *King James 11* on the Down *Cornish Riviera Express* picking up water at speed whilst passing the two header tanks. At a speed of around 70mph the fireman will need to time his lowering and raising of the tender scoop carefully, to avoid damage to the scoop, but still picking up around 2,500gallons. This photo has been cropped to better shew the action, but the photographer will need to beat a hasty retreat having got his shot! Perhaps his plan was to make use of the ladder of the nearby Down Home signal for Fairwood Crossing, although it is unlikely that he could still have climbed fast enough to avoid a soaking!

Long distance trains were routed on the Frome avoiding line at Clink Road Junction, while stopping services would head round through the station having been joined by the Frome & North Somerset line to Bristol via Radstock. With the 5.10pm stopping service from Melksham to Frome, 3689 is passing Frome North Signal Box, which has now been relocated to Didcot Railway Centre and where it carries the earlier name of Frome Mineral Junction Signal Cabin.

FROME

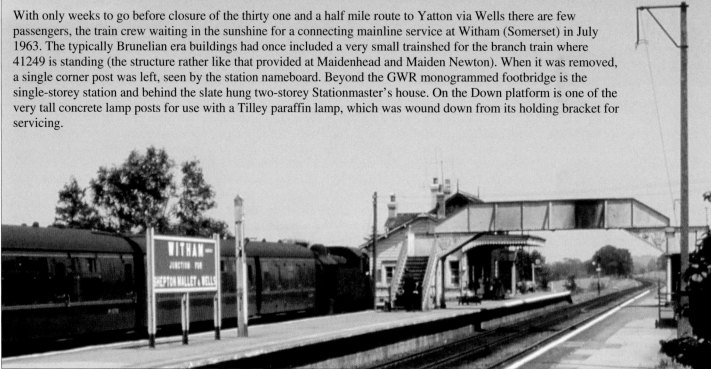

With only weeks to go before closure of the thirty one and a half mile route to Yatton via Wells there are few passengers, the train crew waiting in the sunshine for a connecting mainline service at Witham (Somerset) in July 1963. The typically Brunelian era buildings had once included a very small trainshed for the branch train where 41249 is standing (the structure rather like that provided at Maidenhead and Maiden Newton). When it was removed, a single corner post was left, seen by the station nameboard. Beyond the GWR monogrammed footbridge is the single-storey station and behind the slate hung two-storey Stationmaster's house. On the Down platform is one of the very tall concrete lamp posts for use with a Tilley paraffin lamp, which was wound down from its holding bracket for servicing.

Before the GWR direct line, in 1892-5 Parliamentary approval had been sought for the 'Somerton, Keinton Mandeville, Castle Cary & Evercreech Tramway Syndicate Ltd for a standard gauge line of 14¼miles connecting to this station.

Light engine 25052 heads towards Taunton in July 1978, as the Weymouth line curves away, at the west end of Castle Cary. Of interest here is the WW2 replacement signal box (where No 1729 was destroyed, one of only two GW engines lost to enemy action during the war). The station was attacked on 3 September 1942, perhaps by mistake for the nearby ammunition dump at Alford, resulting in three railwaymen being fatally injured. Behind the box, the corrugated iron section of the goods shed was built on to the brick remnants. Machine gun holes in the further store were repaired with nuts, bolts and large washers as new material was in short supply.

CASTLE CARY

WITHAM   STRAP LANE HALT   BRUTON   CASTLE CARY   SPARKFORD   MARSTON MAGNA

Around Yeovil

Top left - Following singling of the Weymouth line from Castle Cary in 1968, operations were controlled using the electric key token system, this well stocked operating machine being in a shed at Castle Cary. **Top right -** At Yeovil Pen Mill, a diverted Up west of England HST is seen passing the former cattle pens on the left, whilst to the right a footpath now runs beside the alignment of the route to Yeovil Town and Taunton. In the 'V' of the two lines, was the GW Loco Shed closed when the line came under SR control and the allocation moved to their shed beside Town station.

Left - Facing back towards Pen Mill, this is Clifton Maybank Junction Signal Box in 1928 with the line behind the box curving around to go under the SR mainline and up to the Transfer Shed (**Lower right**) now part of the Yeovil Railway Centre. Notice how this line betrays its broad gauge origins, still having baulk road track. This section closed in 1937. The bridge in the centre was the chord for SR traffic between Yeovil and Templecombe. (Wallis coll.) To ease wartime working a new link was installed between the GW and SR to the north of the SR main line, controlled by South Junction Signal Box whose interior is seen **inset.**

Above – As is evident here, Maiden Newton station is on the edge of the town, the SR signals are prominent and behind them is the Bridport Branch trainshed. Branch trains had used the gravity run round siding on the raised bank to the right. 34102 *Lapford* is heading for Westbury with a train of Channel Island produce from Weymouth in early summer 1967,

Right + inset - In its last days, the branch was but a bleak shadow of its former self, with a single car unit at the terminus and closure notice at Toller in May 1975. Camping out here on the night before closure, I recall only too well how bleak it was!

PUBLIC NOTICE
PASSENGER SERVICE
MAIDEN NEWTON - BRIDPORT

BRIDPORT

Bradford Peverell & Stratton Halt over thirty years after closure in 1966, and subsequent singling of the line.   P Triggs coll A Crump

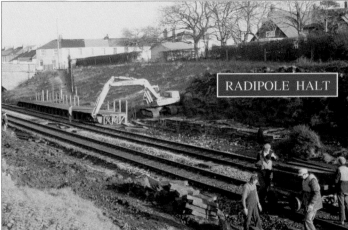

RADIPOLE HALT

For steam enthusiasts, the climb from Weymouth to Bincombe could produce spectacular results, heavier trains requiring banking. **Above left** - Bincombe Tunnel Signal Box looks out over the centre siding provided for banking engines awaiting return. Heading down the hill is 34108 *Wincanton* with a Bournemouth Central to Weymouth service on 6 June 1965. **Top right** - demolition of Radipole Halt a former Great Western gem with its pagoda shelters and profusion of signs: February 1984. **Right** - Looking out from the Station Signal Box to the terminus soon to be transformed by the clearance of the last of the old buildings and introduction of the third-rail electric's. Across the empty goods yard, a line of stock is standing on the Quay Tramway. In August 2003 traffic here was being handled by two class 47's, an EMU and a DMU. P Triggs coll A Crump

WEYMOUTH

YEOVIL PEN MILL

THORNFORD BRIDGE HALT

YETMINSTER

CHETNOLE HALT

EVERSHOT

CATTISTOCK HALT

A DAY IN THE CHANNEL ISLANDS

LIMITED RAIL AND MARINE EXCURSION
(Weather and circumstances permitting)

WEDNESDAY, AUGUST 18th
TO
GUERNSEY
(via TORQUAY and BRITISH RAILWAYS' MAIL STEAMER)

FROM	DEPART	Combined Fares (Third Class)	Return Train Arrives
	a.m.	s. d.	(Night) a.m.
EXETER (St. David's)	6 40	}	12 20
EXETER (St. Thomas)	6 44	37/6	12 15
EXMOUTH (via Ferry and Starcross)	6 §30		12 §50
STARCROSS	7 0	35/6	12 5
			p.m.
DAWLISH WARREN	7 5	35/3	11 55
DAWLISH	7 10	35/0	11 50
TEIGNMOUTH	7 20	34/6	11 45
NEWTON ABBOT	7 38	33/9	11 30
	a.m.		
TORQUAY arr.	7 56		
TORQUAY (Haldon Pier) dep.	9 0	BOOK EARLY	
	p.m.		
GUERNSEY (St. Peter Port) arr.	1 30		

RETURN (same day) depart Guernsey (St. Peter Port) 5½30 p.m.

NOTES. §—Passengers from Exmouth travel forward by Devon Dock Pier and S.S.Co's special ferry to Starcross; on the return journey passengers for Exmouth travel by special Devon General Bus from Starcross (Station).

†—Passengers arrive Torquay (Haldon Pier) 10.0 p.m. on the return journey, and proceed by rail from Torquay at 11.15 p.m.

Haldon Pier is approximately thirty minutes' walk from Torquay Station and passengers make their own way at their own expense between the two points. A service of Devon General Omnibuses will operate between Torbay Road (near Torquay Station) and the Strand which is within five minutes' walk of Haldon Pier.

Bookings for this Excursion are strictly limited and may cease on or before 12.0 noon Tuesday, August 17th. Passengers are advised to book well in advance.

MOTOR COACH DRIVE AROUND GUERNSEY (Optional)—Motor Coaches will meet the Steamer at Guernsey for a drive around the Island, visiting places of interest. Tea will be provided at a good class hotel. Inclusive charge for Motor Coach Drive and Tea, 10s. 0d. (Children under 14 years, 7s. 6d.). Tickets for the Motor Coach Drive (including Tea) obtainable on board the Steamer.

Children under Three years of age, Free ; Three and under Fourteen years of age, half-fare.

NOTICE AS TO CONDITIONS.—These tickets are issued subject to the British Transport Commission's published Regulations and Conditions applicable to British Railways exhibited at their Stations or obtainable free of charge at Station Booking Offices.
Tickets can be obtained in advance at Booking Stations and Agencies.

IT WOULD ASSIST THE RAILWAYS IN PROVIDING ADEQUATE ACCOMMODATION
IF INTENDING PASSENGERS WOULD OBTAIN THEIR TICKETS IN ADVANCE.

Further information will be supplied on application to Booking Stations, Agencies, or to Mr. D. H. HAWKESWOOD, District Commercial Superintendent, Exeter (St. David's) (Telephone Exeter 2281, Extension 301, 302 or 303) ; or to Mr. A. C. B. PICKFORD, Commercial Superintendent, Paddington Station, W.2.
Paddington Station, W.2.
July, 1954

Weymouth is as inseparable from its famous quay tramway, now mothballed and largely tarred over, as it is for having the best beach sand for sand castles - enabling a finely crafted model of Bath Abbey **(Lower left)** to be constructed in the summer of 1960 (its namesake engine, 5083 having been withdrawn the previous year). The Great Western Marine Dept had long been very much a part of the town with its proud flag flying from the mast of a succession of cross channel steamers **(Inset opposite page).** Best known of these were probably the RMS's St Helier and St Julien, both built in 1925. Following war service, which included being some of the very last ships to take men to safety from Dunkirk, they were refurbished, and eventually withdrawn in 1959/60. **Above -** Looking down the River Wey in 1959, the tramway is on the left. Tied up and out of use is one of the former GW steamers now with a buff funnel. **Below -** Most other GW ships saw some wartime service, but the SS St Patrick was bombed and sank in service, off Fishguard, her replacement is at Weymouth in August 1961, with her funnel in buff rather than the previous owners red. **Left -** A 1954 handbill is worth a closer look, including passengers from Exmouth via Starcross who would miss their last ferry home and have to take a Devon General bus!

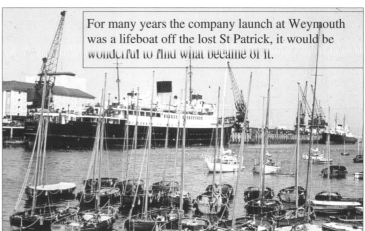

For many years the company launch at Weymouth was a lifeboat off the lost St Patrick, it would be wonderful to find what became of it.

For those not on the Weymouth Slip of days gone by, the train would be racing on towards Taunton, over the largely downhill and level route through Somerton and Langport East. This is perhaps an appropriate moment to consider the train in rather different settings, starting with Arnold Ridley's film 'The Ghost Train' of 1931. Aside of the ghost train itself (being used as a cover for gun running), The *Cornish Riviera Express* is the other principal train in the action. For the film, scenes were shot with 5006 *Tregenna Castle* on the Reading - Basingstoke line, between Reading - Didcot, and on the Radstock - Mells Road section, with most of the action taking place at the closed Dunkerton Colliery Sidings and Camerton station. These scenes used a Dean Goods and 5006 was replaced by a Mogul! For the film, Camerton was altered, refurbished and renamed Fal Vale a fictitious junction for Truro! The best known scene of the ghost train running off an open swing bridge required the use of Barmouth Bridge - surely the only time coaches appeared there with Cornish Riviera roofboards. On a gentler note, the section from Paddington to Taunton was regularly used by the composer Vivien Ellis, inspiring him to compose a piece which very regrettably was turned down when offered to the GWR, only to be snapped up by the LMS, becoming their theme tune '*The Coronation Scot*'. Its wonderful melody sounds all the better, knowing it was inspired by a King class loco!

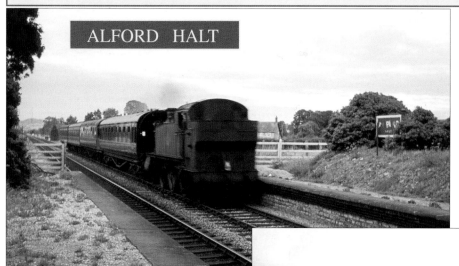

ALFORD HALT

Above + Inset - Just over three miles west of Castle Cary was Alford MOD sidings on the Down side and half a mile later was Alford Halt. With a Centenary Stock vehicle as the second coach, 4143 rolls to a stand with the last Castle Cary to Taunton local on 8 September 1962. No passengers await, but rearranging the letters of the nameboard has provided some local entertainment. The last corresponding Up working was handled by Hymek D7045.

Right - A single chimney King as immaculate as its rake of matching stock shews how its done when given a clear road in this evocative view from c1956 of the *Cornish Riviera* at Keinton Mandeville.

Somerton, like all stations west of Castle Cary, other than Athelney, (which retained services on the Taunton-Yeovil line until that too closed in 1964) closed on the same day, the canopy-less building remained for use by PW staff fifteen years later.

Above - Creech St Michael Halt Up side on the four track section through Taunton.
Below - Dating from 1931, Cogload Flyover is not noted for its beauty. Looking south, the Up Bristol line is almost hidden in the foreground, the Down line being carried over the flyover. Castle Cary is away to the left and Creech Troughs a mile further right towards Taunton.

MAIDEN NEWTON

GRIMESTONE & FRAMPTON

BRADFORD PEVERELL & STRATTON HALT

DORCHESTER WEST

MONKTON & CAME HALT

UPWEY WISHING WELL HALT

An everyday scene with 6157 bringing a local service of ex Great Western stock, in to Taunton in January 1962. Yard shunting is watched over by the signalman of East Loop Signal Box. To the left, is the Engineers Depot (behind which was the Concrete Works, beyond, the Bridge Yard and stabling shed for the Divisional Inspection Saloon), in their siding is an old Toplight mess coach, two ex ROD and a Dean/Churchward 3000 gallon tenders forming the division weed-killing train. On the left one of the first series Hymek's, (D7000-18) just creeps in. In the early days of the station there had been a level crossing here: from by the black building to Firepool which is beyond this end of the signal box. Until the late 1920s Taunton had also been the Divisional 'Garden Centre' for station garden requisites, although no definite location has yet been found, interestingly there had been the 'Gardeners Arms' pub near to part of the Concrete Works so perhaps that establishment had expanded over the old nursery?

4663 awaits departure from the Chard Bay, 8 September 1962.
M Warburton

Departure time from Paddington since 21 July 1905, when the Langport cut-off came into use, is replicated at Taunton.
Courtesy R Fell.

Left - In May 1968 clearance of the canopy from the closed centre platform was well under way, in the foreground the empty space is the top of the old stairwell. D1002 Western Explorer is on an Up ECS working.

Right - As part of the Exeter MAS scheme, considerable rationalisation took place to what was still largely steam era infrastructure. The array of semaphore brackets and gantries have been cleared along with connections to the Up sidings and Minehead arrival bay. The Down bays and Lifting Shop remain and the Goods Avoiding line has been refurbished. Today there has been considerable further retrenchment. 10 May 1986. M Warburton

Left - Where the photographer is standing at Forty Steps footbridge (now demolished), is within yards of the mid-point between Paddington and Penzance, both of which were just over 163 miles away travelling via Bristol. With changes consequent upon the various cut-off's the half-way point is now near to Whiteball.).

Below right- The Minehead Bay lays empty in the foreground, *Taunton West Station Box* has gone from the end of the centre platform, to be replaced by electrical cabinets. Like *Taunton East Junction*, *West Station Box* had different names on the front and rear – only one side included the word *Signal* on the nameplate. Beyond 50 030 *Repulse*, a class 08 shunter and track machines are stabled in front of the old Lifting Shop whose hoist had long gone by July 1987.

Two views from a passing passenger train on the goods avoiding loop - a rare occurrence. Prominent in the top view is the Coal Stage ramp in blue engineers brick at the end of which is the loading platform which had once supported a 35,000 gallon water tank is in red brick - each of which was marked GWR in the frog. To the left is the entrance to the roundhouse, the Sand Dryer, (beside the 08) Lifting Shop and in the distance, the original down side passenger station building. When the brick building behind the telegraph pole was cleared, many of its fittings were recovered to form the new information office at Didcot Railway Centre.

Just visible in the shed entrance is one of the two ex GWR oil tank wagons that were used for fuel storage, these contained 3108 gallons, a figure that was misinterpreted one day when it was assumed to mean 3180!

The lower view was taken passing over Station Road looking in to the demolished roundhouse where the turntable surround can be seen. All of this, along with the pair of railway houses on the left has now been cleared and landscaped.
Both M Boddy

Below - For many, a surprising objection to reopening of the Minehead branch, came from Western National bus drivers who feared that the railway reopening would potentially put them out of a job. All the more bizarre, in that many of them were members of a railway trade union. Another legacy of Western National's origins in the Great Western Road Motor Dept was the continuing delivery of parcels by bus, a practice started very early on by the GWR and which survived until at least the 1970s, as advertised here on Bristol LH 1571. No TUO 265J seen on a Minehead service in May 1971.

OUR LOCAL EXPRESS
TAUNTON TO MINEHEAD

Above - one of a series of Edwardian humorous cards published by Cynicus and overprinted with local names, in this case Taunton to Minehead. Other local examples noted include Taunton to Barnstaple and Tiverton to Hemyock. This rustic branch line image is rather at odds with the appearance of Crowcombe in The Beatles film *Hard Days Night,* supposedly part of the boys journey from Liverpool to London!

NORTON FITZWARREN

Right - Norton Fitzwarren and across the weed strewn site of the down loop, crowds throng the footbridge to witness the West Somerset Railway's first passenger train to run from and to British Rail metals. This was the *Quantock Explorer* hauled by 47457 on 16 June 1990.

CHARLTON MACKRELL — SOMERTON — LONG SUTTON & PITNEY — LANGPORT EAST — ATHELNEY — CREECH ST MICHAEL HALT

Norton Fitzwarren seen reduced to a shadow of its former self. Milepost 165¼ was unusually, double-sided being in the 'V' of the junction of the Barnstaple branch - it can just be seen opposite the fourth coach of this 'Western' hauled up train. In the foreground is the footprint of the station, the white house once having been the 'Railway Hotel'. The Minehead branch curves off right whilst the bare ballast of the Barnstaple Branch is in the centre. This area, connected to the fields on the left via a culvert, is now part of a triangle created to provide turning facilities for the WSR. On the down side, bare ballast marks the down relief line which had ended opposite the point remains, the connection to the down main being protected by a catch point and headshunt as far as the culvert (just beyond the hedge). It was here in the early hours of 4 November 1940 that 6028 *King George VI* went through the catch point and so running out of track, the loco bogie hit the culvert wall and caused the engine to turn over into the field with six of the thirteen coaches strewn across all lines. Services were diverted via Dulverton and the Exe Valley until single line working could be implemented. P Triggs coll A Crump. **Below images** - The sheared off whistle top was found in the field by a Tiverton schoolboy and used as a doorstop! The replacement bogie on 6028 at the end of her days, it was a rivet from the original that hit a passing train. B Harding 290. Contemporary newspaper hoarding from the Great Western Trust collection at Didcot.

Fireman Seabridge along with twenty seven passengers died in the crash, Driver Stacey subsequently remained on shed duties, never wanting to refer to this incident. Despite being held to blame, it has since been published that signals were reversed on him once, if not twice on leaving Taunton.

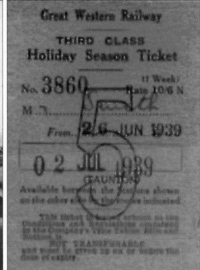

Great Western Railway

THIRD CLASS
Holiday Season Ticket

No. 3860

From 26 JUN 1939

0 2 JUL 1939

TAUNTON

Above - 7317 with an eight coach working steams through Bishops Lydeard where the Signalman is waiting with the key token for the next section to Crowcombe, ready for exchange with the Fireman. Also on the platform is a range of barrows and a chalked notice for a South Wales excursion. With coal, goods and parcels traffic evident, all is well

Left - Elsewhere on the same 8 July 1961, is 4644 passing Leigh Bridge Signal Box between Crowcombe and Stogumber. Highlighted against the second coach is one of the Whitaker automatic token exchangers as were also used on the Somerset & Dorset. This equipment was installed on both the Barnstaple and Minehead branches in the 1930s.
Both M Warburton

Left - Moving to Stogumber on the same day, 6155 has at least eight coaches on a Taunton working. In the yard the Camping Coach made for a popular, inexpensive holiday. Note the campers have their washing hanging out - are they aware it will soon be covered in smuts? Further along beyond the station is the station water supply - a water tank wagon, also a goods van. Laying abandoned under the hedge by the roadside is what appears to be an Austin Seven.

MINEHEAD

Right – Your carriage awaits, but not for long. The 2 January 1971 brought yet another closure and here the sun is setting on what will be the last day of service in public ownership. Tomorrow the platforms built for trainloads of excursionists, will become disused - that is until the efforts of the embryonic West Somerset Railway come to fruition….. .
Both M Warburton

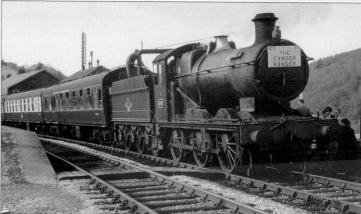

DULVERTON
CHANGE FOR
EXE VALLEY LINE

Left - 1421 takes water at Dulverton before heading back down the Exe Valley to Tiverton and Exeter. Meanwhile passengers wait for a Barnstaple bound train. When that arrives, there is likely to be a delay waiting to pass a Taunton train. With the signal box located beyond the goods shed, an auxiliary key token machine was installed in the small hut at the base of the down starter signal, to reduce delays in crossing times.

Top right - The *Exmoor Ranger* of 27 March 1965 was the last train to traverse some lines, and the last steam to be seen on others. Headed by 3205 the service has stopped for water, before heading for Taunton (becoming the last steam engine to use the shed which closed that day) before returning to Exeter.

Top left - The front of the auxiliary token hut features while 7333 has her safety valves lifting in readiness for the climb to the highest point on the line near East Anstey, much of it at 1 in 60 or steeper. Leading Brake 3rd is W4069 dating from 1936, but still looking very smart in September 1962.

Barnstaple Junction

Left - Leaving Barnstaple Loop to join the Southern on the approach to Barnstaple Junction where a Bulleid West Country has steam to spare, standing next to the dilapidated wooden loco shed. Although the line is curving left here, trains for Ilfracombe will then swing sharp right to cross the Taw beside the large brick building of furniture manufacturer Shapland & Petter.

Moguls of the 53xx type, such as train engine 5336, were becoming a rarity by May 1964, the Barnstaple Branch being one of their last stamping grounds.

Right - Time for a final check around and oil top up for 6340 before leaving Barnstaple Junction for the slog to Mortehoe, on what appears to be an excursion, Whit Monday 1961.
G Robinson coll A Crump

ILFRACOMBE SLIPS
MINEHEAD +
TAUNTON

BISHOPS
LYDEARD

CROWCOMBE

STOGUMBER

WILLITON

WATCHET

With the tide out in Barnstaple Bay, Warship D865 *Zealous* rumbles over Taw Bridge towards Barnstaple Town, and eventually Ilfracombe. Great Western influence is to be found in the lead vehicle which displays the distinctive outline of DW139 the 'Whitewash Coach' officially the 'Track Testing Car'. Built in 1911, transferred to the Experimental Section in 1928 and eventually withdrawn in 1989, this historic vehicle is part of the National Collection but currently remains neglected and in store. Given that this picture has been dated to circa June 1970 it seems unlikely that anyone was considering track improvements when the line was due to close from 5 October. Today the water still eddies around the pier bases.

Left - The 08.50 Taunton to Ilfracombe headed by Mogul 6343 near Braunton. After a slight dip near Wrafton, it would be a continuous climb for most of the next six and a half miles, nearly half being at 1 in 40, hence the frequent use of banking engines from Braunton. On the return, crews were faced with two miles at 1 in 36, a real challenge for the less than sure-footed Bulleid West Country class!

Above - Confusingly carrying the headcode for the 21.25 Plymouth - Truro, D865 *Zealous* is ready for the 18.10 return from Ilfracombe to Exeter. With only a few months left before final closure all the carriage sidings (left) and goods yard (right) have been lifted.

Right - By the summer of 1959 the days of paddle steamers were numbered, PS *Cardiff Queen* would see out a couple more seasons along this coast, eventually ending her days at Cashmores, Newport. With the loss of coastal trippers, and then the railway too, the town has still not recovered its tourism trade.

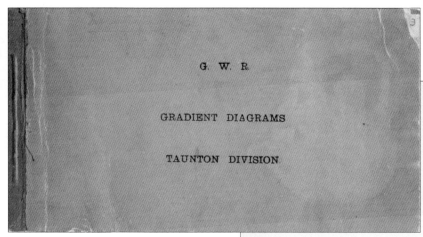

The challenge of the gradients beyond Newton Abbot are well known, although as can be seen here, the section from Taunton to Whiteball had its trials too. Soon after Wellington the grade stiffens from 1 in 90 to 1 in 86, then 1 in 80 before easing to 1 in 127 through the tunnel, the summit being just beyond. From Exeter the two miles of 1 in 115 show that in 1904 *City of Truro* had every opportunity to achieve a high speed on her descent to Wellington, even if the reported figure of 102 mph may not be totally accurate. This book of Gradient Diagrams originated from Swindon Works Drawing Office and was for use in the Divisional Inspection Saloon.

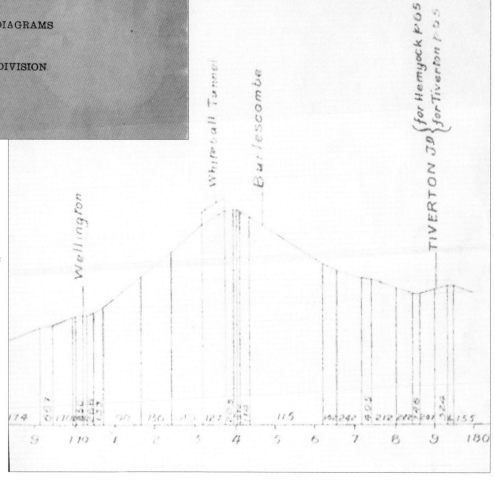

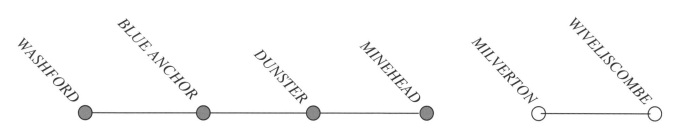

45

Formerly D1685 but now running as 47098, approaching the site of Victory Siding Signal Box, the siding of the same name having been on the right. Also, to the right of the telegraph poles is one of the places where the line of the old Grand Western Canal can be seen. Taunton's goods loop was built on the canal which continues parallel at this point, then crossing and recrossing the railway - a short section at Nynehead now holds water again - before reappearing as a proper waterway near Burlescombe. The overhead pylons are just beyond the old Barnstaple branch as it heads off towards Milverton. Opening of the Langport cut-off required revision of the arrangements for mail traffic from Millbay to Bristol and the North. Instead of it being slipped as the train passed through Bedminster, it was now to be slipped here at Victory Crossing. P Triggs coll A Crump

WELLINGTON (SOM)

Above - Another class 47, passing the old station yard and cattle pens with a headshunt through the Goods Shed - which remained out of use for at least a decade up to the mid seventies.

Below - Turning 180°, a class fifty is approaching past the corner of the Goods Shed. This remarkable survivor remains, having been in industrial use for nearly half a century and is a survivor from the original station, unlike the signalbox and up side waiting room which were of 1930s vintage. The latter was used by the local PW men until both were swept away in the 1980s.

Interloper 60532 *Blue Peter* with a rake of green SR stock on the LCGB *A2 Commemorative Railtour* which it worked from Waterloo via Exeter (stalling on Honiton Bank), seen here descending Whiteball, at Beam Bridge where it was nearly three hours late! 18 August 1966. However, aside of the rather bizarre combination of motive power, stock and route, there is much else of interest here. Engineers are replacing the deck of the A38 road bridge and their speed restriction (opposite the end cottage) would have been yet more of a hold up for *Blue Peter*. It appears they also have possession of the down line where a crane is attending. When the Bristol & Exeter Railway were building their line, they opened a temporary terminus here at Beam Bridge, pending completion of Whiteball Tunnel and the line to Exeter, the work finished on 1 May 1844. The site of the temporary terminus would have been somewhere near where the photographer is standing, but is difficult to pinpoint as the A38 road has been realigned over the years. During the time this (temporary) station was operating, a stage coach service ran to Exeter, handbills for which were found in the attic of one of the cottages just before they were pulled down some years ago. A pile of them having been used to form a comfortable nest by a small rodent - obviously a rail enthusiast! Sadly although most disintegrated, one was saved and placed in the Somerset County Records Office. Unfortunately on trying to obtain a copy to include here, it could not be found. In 1904 *City of Truro* came past this point at somewhere near the recorded speed of 102.34 mph before having to brake for PW men on the track nearer Wellington.

WHITEBALL TUNNEL
NORTH END

Sweeping around the curve from Beam Bridge and on up through Marlands, 5032 *Usk Castle* heads for home at Newton Abbot with the *Torbay Express*. Being a very long 'pull' for the Whiteball Signalman, this Distant signal was replaced by a colour light around the end of the 1950s. As No 5032 has been fitted with a double chimney (July 1959), the view must be soon after that date. Taunton had several 41xx prairies allocated for banking at Wellington, indeed well in to the diesel era, a 'Hymek' was to be found parked in the down loop at Wellington awaiting its next call. Banking engines would come off at the summit where refuge sidings were provided.

VEN CROSS ○——— MOREBATH ○——— MOREBATH JUNCTION HALT ○——— DULVERTON ○——— EAST ANSTEY ○——— YEO MILL HALT ○

Above - The King of locomotives as she (he) was justifiably referred to by the GWR, 6000 *King George V* shows what a King could do, taking a heavily laden train up the 1 in 80 with barely a wisp of exhaust and safety valves lifting while the Fireman has a break - truly both men and machine are masters of their job! The commemorative bell also appears to be ringing in time with the cylinder beats! Again, this is Marlands, in the cutting leading to the tunnel.

Right - Whiteball Tunnel is a well known landmark, but how many ever get to look at the land above the tunnel? Whiteball was created by an army of around one thousand navvies who dug a number of shafts, before connecting these up at a cost of £59 per cubic yard. Spoil from the workings can still be seen from a public footpath that runs over the top, across an area known as 'The Tippings', now rather overgrown but sheltering a fine array of bluebells in Spring. Currently, there is much interest in the creation of '*The Whiteball Tunnel Heritage Trail*' which aims to reconnect the two local sections of the Grand Western Canal via this footpath, highlighting along the way, some of the history of this area; the Navvies, the construction, and of course *City of Truro*'s high speed run.

Wellington Monument

To Beam Bridge, Whiteball and Marlands

On 28 April 1912, Odette Brailly was born in Amiens France, having married she moved to London in 1932. With three young girls, life was difficult in the blitz of 1940, and in October Odette moved with her children to the peace of Devon, at Redball. This also brought her close to her elderly and unwell mother-in-law at Whiteball, whom she visited and cared for daily. It was not long before she found an alternative route for her commute, the footpath that runs through Marlands and over the tunnel. Having a great appreciation of the wonders of nature, this is the view that she would have enjoyed from the top of The Tippings, a panorama of the Blackdown Hills from above Taunton to Hackpen Hill in the Culm Valley. Central is Culmstock Beacon which still has a Beacon Keepers hut (arrowed). After the London Blitz, this landscape had a pivotal effect , '*...with all her heart she wished that her body could in some way be dedicated to these most beloved fields...*' (*Odette*, Jerrard Tickell, Chapman & Hall London 1949 p49). It was initially by accident that she came to the attention of the wartime Special Operations Executive, who quickly realised the potential of her knowledge, personality and ability. So it was that after a period of intensive training she again found herself passing here on the *Cornish Riviera Express* en route to Plymouth and shortly after, Portreath from where the RAF were to get her to France. Four attempted flights failed and so finally the journey was undertaken by sea, to begin a new life as a British Agent in Occupied France. Eventually betrayed in April 1943, she was imprisoned for the rest of the war under terrible conditions enduring repeated Gestapo interrogations and torture. One of the lucky few to survive she returned to England on VE Day, although medical opinion was such that she was unlikely to live long as her health was now so poor. Desperately in need of rest and recuperation, she returned to this area, to a cottage on Culmstock Beacon. It was while she was here that she learned that she had become the first woman to be awarded the George Cross for her bravery.

Culmstock Beacon

To Redball, Burlescombe and Exeter

Her immensely moving story became more widely known as a result of various books published over the years, and the hugely popular 1950 film '*Odette*' starring Anna Neagle, Peter Ustinov and Trevor Howard, although it has never previously been associated with the spoil heaps of Whiteball Tunnel where it had all begun! Within the commemorative markers of the previously referred to *Whiteball Tunnel Heritage Trail* it is also intended to record Odette's love of, and dedication to these hills. (For those users of modern-day road-motors, the M5 motorway now passes through the middle of this pastoral scene, being hidden in a fold of the hill). Fortunately 1945 medical opinion was incorrect and Odette recovered to survive until 1995.

BISHOPS NYMPTON & MOLLAND ○——— SOUTH MOLTON ○——— FILLEIGH ○——— SWIMBRIDGE ○——— BARNSTAPLE JUNCTION SR ○——— BARNSTAPLE TOWN SR ○

Right + inset- just outside the tunnel is the remains of the Down Engineers siding and workmen's cabin.

Taunton Engineers Dept had their own vehicle DW14955 specially built as a tunnel inspection vehicle - sadly one gem that went to Woodhams scrapyard at Barry and wasn't saved. On the top left of the tunnel mouth is a very weathered patch of whitewash to improve vision in the days of semaphore signalling. Above the tunnel, a levelled area is one of the shaft sites - these were all filled in after completion of the tunnel. Work has just been completed on Phase One of relining the tunnel with concrete sprayed over mesh on much of the upper half, later in 2014 concrete panels will be bolted to the lower half. Pictures courtesy Network Rail.

WHITEBALL TUNNEL—SOUTH END

Lower left - 47471 breasts the summit with The Tippings extending over the hill in the centre (the tunnel itself is straight but approached by curves at both ends). To the right the down relief line was opened in 1927 - see opposite. Just beyond the overbridge is the front of Whiteball Siding Signal Box.

WRAFTON SR ○— BRAUNTON SR ○— MORTEHOE & WOOLACOMBE SR ○— ILFRACOMBE SR ○   NORTON FITZWARREN ○— WELLINGTON ○

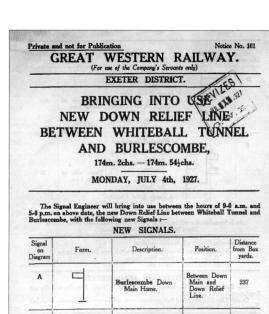

GREAT WESTERN RAILWAY.

(For use of the Company's Servants only)

EXETER DISTRICT.

BRINGING INTO USE NEW DOWN RELIEF LINE BETWEEN WHITEBALL TUNNEL AND BURLESCOMBE,

174m. 2chs. — 174m. 54½chs.

MONDAY, JULY 4th, 1927.

The Signal Engineer will bring into use between the hours of 9-0 a.m. and 5-0 p.m. on above date, the new Down Relief Line between Whiteball Tunnel and Burlescombe, with the following new Signals :—

NEW SIGNALS.

Signal on Diagram	Form.	Description.	Position.	Distance from Box yards.
A		Burlescombe Down Main Home.	Between Down Main and Down Relief Line.	237
B		Burlescombe Down Relief Line to Down Main Home.	Down side of Relief Line.	237
C		Whiteball Tunnel Down Main Advanced Starting with lower Inner Distant Arm for Burlescombe.	Between Down Main and Down Relief Line.	454

Top right - With the down loop now cut back to Whiteball, an Engineers train awaits a path while D173 accelerates past with the 11.20 Plymouth to Manchester July 1972. On the skyline is the pink scar of the face of Westleigh Quarry, rail connected by the Bristol & Exeter Rly to supply their ballast. Two 3' gauge engines known as *The Little Dutchmen* were used to propel wagons from the interchange sidings to the quarry. (The name related to the then West of England expresses, *Zulu* and *The Flying Dutchman*). S Hookins coll A Crump

BURLESCOMBE and the Westleigh Quarry Tramway.
An 1898 diagram of the twenty-five year old 3' gauge line built by the B & E R (dark blue line) and its standard gauge replacement (pink) built with second hand - ex broad gauge material - supplied by the GWR whose main line runs top to bottom on the left. The station was just off the lower corner. Note the 3' gauge loco shed on the canal bank, much of that line was on a timber trestle viaduct about twenty feet high. On at least two occasions, derailments led to engines landing in the field below! Rail traffic ended in the early 1950s and gradually the rails were lifted for use in the quarry stone hoppers. Fortunately some rail and pointwork survived long enough to be recovered by the Great Western Society, Taunton Group.

BURLESCOMBE

Previous page, clockwise - A montage of the tramway which went out of use c1951 having been operated by only two engines, as was the B & E R system previously (the quarry also had their own internal 3' system and a variety of interesting engines). **Top left -** Initial clearance work, with the main line through the gap in the hedge, as seen in 1978 (C Honnor). **Top right -** A view towards the quarry. **Lower right -** Bridge over the canal, made of two pairs of early curved top girders - direct descendants of the tubes of the Royal Albert Bridge and visible from passing trains. **Lower left -** Last remnants of a wagon. All Chris Tilley **Right** - After spending a year uncovering the fascinating remains of the system, the items were recorded and moved to Didcot Railway Centre where relaid, they now form a unique display of broad and mixed gauge trackwork, home to replica engines *Fire Fly* and *Iron Duke*. The nameboard recalls this legacy.

Tiverton Parkway

Whilst the B & E R were planning their line, they were petitioned to provide a station for the town of Tiverton at what became Tiverton Junction, rather than Sampford Peverell as the road from Tiverton was so dangerous (There had been a number of accidents with runaway horse drawn waggons). Eventually the GWR did open an additional halt in 1928, never very well used, it closed from 5 October 1964. Construction of the North Devon Link Road from nearby J27 on the M5 led to the closure of Tiverton Junction and construction of the new Tiverton Parkway on the former halt site, which opened 12 May 1986. The North Devon Link Road soon gained its own unenviable reputation for serious accidents, particularly on the stretch to Tiverton which now has a central crash barrier fitted.

SAMPFORD PEVERELL HALT

TIVERTON JUNCTION
CHANGE FOR
TIVERTON, EXE VALLEY
CULM VALLEY BRANCHES

37
FROM
HEMYOCK
FACING

DOWN
PLATF'M

Even before more recent rationalisations which have seen the demise of the oil storage facility and even more track, the location was hardly recognisable.

Above - Taken a week after closure to passengers of the Culm Valley branch (curving away right), D867 *Zenith* of Laira has what looks like a Gresley vehicle at the head of its thirteen coaches. On the Up platform a relief crew wait their charge - note the Driver with his 'Grimsby box', joined by the crew of the *Tivvy Bumper* who have just topped up 1450 now impatient to propel auto-trailer W223W back to Tiverton. Much loved sister engine 1442 can be found nearby in Tiverton Museum.
M Warburton **Right -** The M5 with its artificial hump over the non existent Hemyock line, has transformed the backdrop of this rural scene.

CULLOMPTON

Left -Cullompton, or Collumpton as it often used to appear, has been largely ignored by photographers, whilst like Wellington it may yet reopen, (it is also now the site of the M5 Services).   M Boddy

KENSHAM SIDING

Below -A broad gauge era plan shews a mixed gauge goods shed and siding, viewed today there is little but dense undergrowth, the access road on the plan has vanished completely. The unusual feature of this facility, was that a goods only station was a great rarity on the GWR, it was only a mile from Hele & Bradninch and had no obvious potential for traffic apart from a modest paper mill some way off (which after a succession of major fires closed at around the time the goods shed was removed c1897). The siding remaining for some years for engineers use and a Royal Train visit to the nearby Duchy town of Bradninch by King Edward V111 in June 1936, The level crossing went many years ago, but its remnant can still be seen as an emergency access point to the southbound M5.

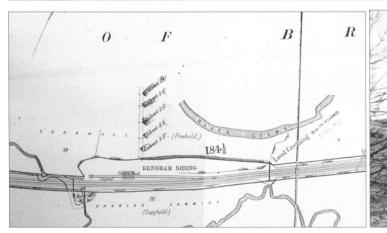

SILVERTON

Above - Silverton Mill siding is largely extant as the rails were set in concrete, the out of use wagon weighbridge seen here continuing to deteriorate. Prior to this branch being built, early edition OS maps confirm there was previously an internal system. Local legend has it that a locomotive used fell into a lime pit where it was abandoned.

Right - The station itself had staggered platforms either side of this bridge at Ellerhayes. In Victorian times the Stationmaster had an Observatory and made an early model of the moon surface. Again, locally there are stories that the Acland family of Killerton House had a separate platform a little to the North just so they did not have to mix with the lesser mortals, but no documentary evidence has yet come to light. (A similar arrangement *is* known to have occurred at Powderham). There is evidence however, for the reason why this is the only bridge on the B & E R to have decorative keystones in its arch. The local press tells us that there was a delay in starting work on the line, and to avoid undue hardship to the Mason's, they were put to work at Killerton. In appreciation, the Mason's left their mark on the bridge nearest to the house in the form of 'a bird in hand' - the crest of Sir Thomas Acland. Much later the Acland's had their own railway, in the form of a portable system for use with their estate sawmill. This was disposed of when the National Trust took over and eventually became part of the new Seaton Electric Tramway.

Right lower - passing the break section signal box at Rewe, in use 'as required' from 1934-64. With a rake of ex GW stock, 6375 is about to go under Columbjohn bridge c1960 at a time when this was a Taunton loco.

Inset - Shelf plate from Stoke Canon Crossing Signal Box.

REWE

Right - Closed Stoke Canon Crossing Signal Box boarded up following closure in 1985. Although listed as an Historic Building, this Saxby & Farmer box which dates from prior to the GWR takeover of the B & E R in 1876, has been wantonly neglected and damaged. Previous attempts to give it a better future have been thwarted but it is to be hoped that it can still be saved. The station here was another with staggered platforms, the Exe Valley line opened in 1885, at its junction quarter of a mile to the west a replacement station opened in 1894.

Cowleybridge Junction has been much in the news over recent years because of flooding of the main line. This has led to provision of inflatable barriers put across the line to deflect water back to the river. Christmas traffic was recently disrupted by such a deployment-in spite of the fact that there was no floodwater in sight!

COWLEY

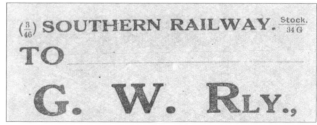

Left - When the lines to Crediton and North Devon were being planned and built, they too were much in the news. Too complex to cover here, it led to the construction of a temporary station at Cowley on the Crediton line - later removed to Newton St Cyres, because of the unwillingness of the B & E R to accept the LSWR in to Exeter St Davids. Connection to the city was to be by carriage, the road connection being along the line of the current overhead cables. The station itself was beside where the modern day unit is - between the clump of bushes and river bridge (highlighted in red).

Left - Press reports at the opening of the line on 1 May 1844 suggested that Resident Engineer William Froude had produced such a wonderful spectacle in the brickwork of the skew arch at Cowley, that it would become a major tourist attraction if it didn't fall down! 45029 would seem excessive power for a single Presflo cement wagon. The brick building through the arch, is the switchgear room that suffers during local flooding.

Below - A halt that doesn't appear in the timetable, but is a well known landmark beside the railway approaching Exeter.

Left - From Exeter St Davids is a stiff incline to Central, for which the heavy steam era trains required banking. The coming of the LSWR also brought about the need for the Transfer Shed centre distance and hopefully to be put to use again. Z class 30956 is returning to the bankers siding just beyond the Red Cow Crossing. For some reason classmate 30954 was always known by enginemen here as *Dolly*. 1 October 1962. M Warburton

SILVERTON   STOKE CANON   EXETER ST DAVIDS   ST THOMAS   EXMINSTER   STARCROSS

Right - By the end of March 1985 work was well underway on track and signalling alterations for the next phase of M.A.S. Gone are the banking engines siding and much of the freight traffic, Exeter Middle Signal Box would close at the end of the day and already the nameplate has disappeared. At the end of the platform, Red Cow Crossing is being relaid. Had the GWRs 1930s plans come to fruition, a high level station was to be built for SR trains, which would take them over Riverside Yard and along separate track to Cowley Bridge Junction. The pale green painted building was the GWR Cadbury distribution depot.
M Warburton

Left -The frontage dates from 1864 with additions of 1938.

Right - How many times have we taken part in, or seen such a race along the platform-before current safety concerns became so constricting! Running neck and neck a young athlete and D1058 *Western Nobleman* speed west together through St Davids: the train on the Down Through line. Above the engine is the clerestory which has since been covered in - a carryover from the days when the frontage supported a vast overall roof 363' x 132'.

At the top of St Davids Hill, a well known landmark is the statue of General Buller. Cast at Thames Ditton on the LSWR, it was the GW who transported and erected it in well under the agreed time! Reputedly, Penguin Books was born as a result of an unsatisfactory visit to the station bookstall in 1935.

Approaching St Davids down the SR bank from Central. Features of note, left to right: the water tank of the gas works (formerly the atmospheric pump house), rear corner of Exeter West Signal Box (now preserved at Crewe Heritage Centre), to the left of the engine was the loco shed yard and Goods Avoiding Line. Dereliction abounds to the right of the station on what was known to the end as South Devon Sidings. Alongside the trackless South Devon Rly carriage shed had been another single track similar structure, thought to have been for 'motive power'. M Boddy **Insets** - The Bristol & Exeter Rly and S D R formed an end on connection here, each with their own distinctive boundary markers.

A view off the platform toward Exeter West a week after closure of the box, 11 May 1985. M Warburton

From St Davids, the crossing of the River Exe provided the location for the earliest known colour shot of a train in motion in July 1934 although the image did not include the narrow-gauge served, adjacent Flowerpot Refuse Tip! Before St Thomas, is currently the GW Staff Association Club, built on the site of the raised goods yard that existed in the early days - the junction location can still be seen.

Always known as St Thomas and one of only two stations on the Western Region to use a bracketed name like this on totem signs. By the Summer of 1970 demolition men had moved in to remove the lovely old overall roof. The sense of history here has been torn away along with the roof, its grandeur now overwhelmed by the oppressive modern buildings around it. Built to be offices for the South Devon, it is currently used as a Chinese restaurant, while passengers at this unstaffed halt have a bus shelter for comfort.   M Warburton

EXETER (ST. THOMAS)

DAWLISH WARREN   DAWLISH   TEIGNMOUTH   SLIPPED AT EXETER   NEWTON ABBOT KINGSWEAR   KINGSKERSWELL   TORRE

EXMINSTER

It was originally proposed that the Exmouth branch would leave the SDR line at 'Exmouth Junction' just North of Exminster, before crossing the river estuary to Topsham and taking up its current route. Wooed by the LSWR the junction was moved to their line to the East of the city. The proposed junction was also close to the starting point for the GWR planned inland route to avoid the coastal section around Dawlish. With earthworks as dramatic as those of the contemporaneous St Germans - Looe branch proposal, there would have been a lengthy tunnel behind Holcombe with another shorter, behind Dawlish, and two similar around Bishopsteignton (see also p 70) . Construction of the avoiding line would have required moving the Exminster water troughs which were along the distant straight in this picture. Viewed in July 1981, the station has long gone, having closed to passengers on 30 March 1964, the platforms once where the bare ballast is seen. To serve the Down Goods Loop, two sidings and Up refuge Siding, the signal box survived until 14 November 1986. Following a period as a bird watchers hide for the adjacent marshland, by September 2006 the condition of the former signal box had deteriorated and consent was given for what was a listed building to be dismantled, with the intention that it would be rebuilt at Broadway on the Gloucester & Warwickshire Rly. This did not happen and tragically, it was destroyed there with rather less publicity than its removal. The semi derelict building on the right is the former SDR station house which was out of use for many years until being taken over by an architectural salvage business.   M Warburton

TURF and the ATMOSPHERIC

Below - The principle of atmospheric traction used a cast iron pipe along the centre of the track, this lengthy section was recovered from under Goodrington Beach, and after extensive conservation work, has been put on display within a track panel at Didcot. Along the top of the tube a continuous slot connected the bottom of the piston carriage to its piston within the tube. Behind the display is a disc & crossbar signal, from the same era, and Frome signal box seen on p62.

Above - Pumping houses every few miles, sucked air out of the tube, drawing the train along. The remains of pumping houses at Starcross, Torquay and Totnes are quite well known, others less so. This is the site at Turf (near Powderham) where the foundations and pond survive, the main line being behind the hedge on the left. Note the mounting bolts. This site was inspected and surveyed by the Broad Gauge Society between 1995-8, (the BGS have also recently brought out a comprehensive book on the various atmospheric railways).

Left - Ultimately the atmospheric system was a failure, partly through failure of the leather valve, but also because of the contractors responsible for its upkeep. Materials from the pump houses were sold off, near Turf, a farm barn appears to be built with stone from the pump house. Other partial remains can be seen passing Dawlish and Rattery. No piston carriages survived as these had the piston removed and then continued in ordinary service. The actual pumping equipment being sold for reuse or scrap.

STARCROSS
for Exmouth

Right - Starcross with its pier and ferry, was for the GWR, the only way to Exmouth, after that towns defection to the LSWR. (Parcels were still sent this way well in to the British Railways era!) The station itself was built as a temporary structure, but survived until 1981, its historic value going unappreciated until too late. The canopy was a cut back remnant of the original overall roof. The Down side shelter had once extended the full length of the white painted railing - doubtless, passengers were grateful for protection from the winds that blow up the estuary. D1036 Western Emperor passes on a sunny 8 May 1976. D Homer coll A Crump

Below left + right - For a time the pump house existed as a museum although now closed, the chimney had been built as roughly double its current height. The footbridge outlived the buildings, lasting over a century before replacement in 1999. M Warburton

The coastal stretch has had its moments of drama, one of the first was when a passing train knocked the bowsprit off a ship at Powderham. The miscreants of one of the first robberies of a mail train also set out from Starcross on New Years Day 1849. Successfully pulling off the theft between Bridgwater and Bristol, they decided to repeat the operation on the return train but were arrested at Bridgwater.

DEVON DOCK, PIER AND STEAMSHIP CO. LTD.

RIVER EXE TRIP (AFTERNOON)

1868

TORQUAY — PRESTON PLATFORM — PAIGNTON — GOODRINGTON SANDS HALT — BROADSANDS HALT — CHURSTON

One of the more unusual, of the many industrial lines associated with this route, was the forestry railway at Starcross. Built by the War Department late in WW1 to move timber out of Mamhead Forest it only lasted a few years, the engine then moving to the railway system at Exeter Gasworks. The standard gauge railway was laid on the road from its connection with the GWR station yard to Mamhead, being worked by a Barclay 0-4-0T loco until the road was returned to public use.

Right - Continuing along the estuary, travellers look out over Exmouth and Holy Trinity church. Between Cockwood Harbour and Dawlish Warren there are extensive mud flats at low tide. A well known landmark here is the wreck of a tramp steamer the 'South Coaster'. Attempting to bring coal to Exeter during WW2 and trying to keep away from U boats, she strayed a little too close to the shore and ran aground near Exmouth. Badly damaged by storms before she could be refloated, this 1916 veteran was eventually towed here and abandoned. Her moment of fame came in more recent times, when a bikini clad figure was seen clinging to the mast - but found by her rescuers to be a shop dummy! Just across the railway were several old carriage bodies from a variety of pre grouping companies including Barry and Metropolitan Railway stock.

The long awaited, first glimpse of the open sea !

During WW2 Dawlish Warren, in common with much of the South Devon coast was at risk of invasion and so beaches were covered with barbed wire. Once cleared after the war, Exeter residents could again take the *Woolworths Express* (fare 6d), to enjoy an evening by the sea. By the early sixties 'trippers' or 'come-by trains' as tourists were known, were beginning to use the motor car - bringing their many caravans with them. Nowadays the caravan park has been covered by amusement arcades, but caravan parks cover vast swathes of the surrounding area so transforming this once peaceful spot. A fleet of Camping Coaches still exists (but with rumours of disposal), their places were previously taken by this magnificent set of ex GWR Toplight vehicles.

THE *Torbay* EXPRESS

FEATURES OF INTEREST EN ROUTE

DAWLISH

Right - With the tide on its way out so making a bit more space for the crowds around Colonnade Viaduct, NBL built Warships D862 *Viking* + D833 *Panther* double head the fifteen coaches of the Down *Cornish Riviera* on 9 June 1963. Initially, the green livery looked very smart on these engines, as on D833, but D862 looks rather too much like it has been left in a pigeon loft and is hardly the image of a railway system trying to attract traffic!   M Warburton

Centre right - Beside Parsons Tunnel the headlands and Parson & Clerk rocks are silhouetted against Dawlish while even a moderate sea shows the dramatic battering that the seawall has been subjected to for so long.

The unique signal box at Dawlish had survived over ninety years of storms and also being machine gunned in WW2, but succumbed to demolition in mid July 2013 in spite of its listing.

For all the problems there have been, much of Brunel's sea wall still remains. Readily seen at Langstone Rock is his curved-face design intended to reduce wave impact. More recently, the Environment Agency were heard to herald their own revolutionary new design 'a sea wall with a curved face to throw back the waves'! **Below -** While mum reads her book oblivious, the boys all have their back to the sea, and even dad looks round for 6013 *King Henry VIII* on the Up *Royal Duchy*. **Right -** Swindon built Warship D806 *Cambrian* on the Down Torbay Express draws rather more interest, being something of a novelty. Both M Warburton, 3 August 1959.

Along the sea wall

Even the GWR's aircraft were given the famous brown and cream livery, the initial service being operated by a hired Westland *Wessex* six-seater, three-engine monoplane registration G AAGW whose image appeared on the air mail stamp. Services were initiated on Wednesday 12 April 1933 using Haldon Airfield with a connecting car service to local stations. For the following summer season, the Big Four railway companies joined forces to form Railway Air Services, using DeHaviland *Dragon* and *Rapide* aircraft. The service moved to Denbury Airfield near Newton Abbot (now HMP Channings Wood) for 1935 and then back to Haldon in 1936-9. Post war RAS became nationalised as BEA and now forms part of British Airways. Haldon under RAS was notable for the fact that it was a request stop, if there were no passengers, a canvas cross was rolled out over the grass and the plane turned away without landing. The very striking first timetable cover was by Charles Mayo.

BRITANNIA HALT ○———— KINGSWEAR ●———— DARTMOUTH ○

TOTNES ●———— KINGSBRIDGE SLIPED AT EXETER / BRENT ○———— AVONWICK ○

When the sidings were lifted on Teignmouth Quay, the rails were found to still be in their SDR rail chairs.

Above - A green Swindon Inter-City unit on an up train under Myrtle Hill bridge, the goods yard which closed in 1967, is on the right. At the time of the atmospheric working, a pump house and reservoir were here but following its demise the area became a rather cramped yard with S & T workshops. **Above right - L**ooking back under neighbouring Shute Hill bridge in September 1971, the Goods Shed and siding have gone, soon to be followed by the signal box which succumbed to Exeter MAS in November 1986. Like many of the resorts along this coast, Teignmouth was made by the railway.

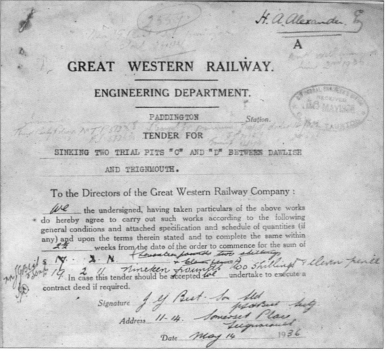

Tender for sinking of trial pits for the inland diversion route tunnel between Dawlish and Teignmouth near what is now *Jack's Patch* which the GWR bought and closed down, dated 14 May 1936, (see page 64).

Once a small village before the coming of the railway, Newton Abbot rapidly expanded as a railway town with its important works and running sheds. Following a major rebuild, opened by Lord Mildmay of Flete, it looked much as per the scene (**Centre right)** with D1002 *Western Explorer* captured n June 1970. The Power Station forms a prominent backdrop. M Warburton. **Centre bottom -** Within the rebuild *Tiny* was plinthed on the platform (now at Buckfastleigh) and Westinghouse signalling installed. The 20 August 1940 brought bombs raining down causing extensive damage. **Top** - No 2785 was badly damaged but eventually returned to service until October 1947, having spent two and a half years in the adjacent repair works! **Bottom left** - Shrapnel holes can still be seen in the canopy around the replacement buildings, behind D1035 *Western Yeoman.* **Centre right –** The loss of the Power Station took considerable coal traffic too, 50 020 *Revenge* heads west past a roofless 3DR building, beyond which are the black and yellow coaches of publishers David & Charles, June 1986. **Bottom right -** Extension of the Exeter MAS scheme implemented in May 1987, has devastated the station and surrounding infrastructure. M Boddy

But I had a bit of a squeeze coming down to TORQUAY.

TORQUAY

Slipping on the through road at Exeter St Davids, the Kingswear portion would then follow on to Aller Junc, before heading down the branch through Kingskerswell and Torre, to Torquay. Summer Saturdays often saw trains backing up to Taunton. Not only were seat reservations essential, at Torquay prospective passengers were not allowed on to the platform until their train was due, in an effort to control the crowds, 'Regulation tickets' were issued with the allocated train number, in advance.

Famous Named Trains
WESTERN REGION

17th SEPTEMBER 1956 to 16th JUNE 1957

BRITISH RAILWAYS

Top - Here, the totem signs along the platforms were made of vinyl, rather than the usual enamelled steel.
Right - On Tuesday 3 September 1963 6936 *Breccles Hall* has just arrived with an Exeter - Kingswear stopper. Note the legacy of the broad gauge era with the extra width between platforms. Post war, proposals for four tracks through Teignmouth were dropped, and work that had started on a new expanded Paignton station was not restarted.
Above - In Edwardian times, Torquay was obviously seen as more of a romantic, rather than a holiday, destination!

GARA BRIDGE   LODDISWELL   KINGSBRIDGE   WRANGATON   BITTAFORD PLATFORM   IVYBRIDGE now on a new site

Right - Changes at Churston. As the 1.50pm Kingswear-Paddington climbs past 'wrong line' led by 5932 *Haydon Hall*, 1466 departs the Brixham bay, a service known locally as the *Brixham whippet*. A fish van in the cattle dock underlines yet more rail traffic that no longer exists.
Below - Run down, reduced to single line only (October 1968) and with the Brixham service gone (May 1963), ownership was transferred away from British Rail in 1972 to become the Torbay Steam Railway. In September 1973 6412 lends colour to a desolate scene. Much development has taken place since with track laid back on the Brixham formation as sidings and a large workshop established on the Up side.

CHURSTON for
BRIXHAM

Even Kings went regularly down the branch to Kingswear such was the importance of this line. On this occasion it is Castle 5043 *Earl of Mount Edgcombe* that has the *Torbay Express* as it draws away from Churston in September 1961. Today No 5043 is highly regarded as a good performer on a variety of steam railtours, having been restored from ex Barry scrapyard condition. The *Torbay Express* is also now run on summer Saturdays from Bristol to Kingswear as a private charter.

Paddington, Exeter, Torquay, Paignton & Kingswear

Left - No more weekdays only *Torbay Express,* (Paddington to Kingswear) *The Devonian* (Bradford-Kingswear), or any through coaches on the *Cornish Riviera Express,* instead Kingswear now has the Torbay Steam Railway where loadings are such that motive power like 4588, has had to been substituted by heavy freight types in pseudo GWR lined green. **Below -** Reliving GWR round tour excursions once again with the coal fired *P S Kingswear Castle.* Among the landmarks to be seen from rail and river are the boatyard of Philip & Son Ltd- builders of the ship in 1924. The yard is on the site of the original rail alignment, bypassed by the Noss Deviation, after which, it had its own siding complex. Currently semi-derelict, it is due to be redeveloped.

KINGSWEAR for DARTMOUTH

GREAT WESTERN RAILWAY
FERRY TICKET.
KINGSWEAR
TO
DARTMOUTH
FARE 1d. C
FOR CONDITIONS SEE BACK
05318

Gt Western Ry.   Gt Western Ry.
DARTMOUTH   DARTMOUTH
TO   (S.5)
TORQUAY
10d. PARLY. (3rd Cls) 10d.
487

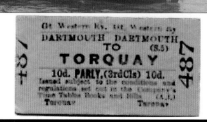

Overlooking the river, and not far from Greenway, is the quiet churchyard of Stoke Gabriel where that great GWR CME George Jackson Churchward is buried in the family grave. A truly great Locomotive Engineer, who influenced so much of twentieth century locomotive design.

Heading west at Dainton, Right – No 34034 *Honiton* and 1930s GW stock. *c*limbing Dainton with an early afternoon Newton Abbot - Plymouth stopper c1957. This was one of the regular workings where WR and SR crews and their respective motive power maintained familiarity with each others routes between Exeter and Plymouth in case of the need for diversions **Below -** 5042 *Winchester Castle* with the Fridays only Paddington-Newquay empty dining cars, falling away towards Totnes on 25 May 1961. Staff would sleep over in old coaches ready for the summer Saturday onslaught. (The GWS 'Dreadnought' coach survived for preservation having been used as sleeping accommodation at Newquay) Taken from Wrigwell Lane bridge, the tunnel mouth is in the background. M Warburton

CORNWOOD ○ — PLYMPTON ○ — LAIRA HALT ○ — LIPSON VALE HALT ○ — MUTLEY ○ — PLYMOUTH NORTH ROAD ●

Right - A closer look at the tunnel mouth shews just how steeply the line falls away from the summit, compared to the sidings that existed both to the left and right of the line. To the right of the 1965 built signal box, was another of the atmospheric pump houses (West of Newton these were not put into regular use). Later the area was used for sidings serving an adjacent quarry and provided a refuge for banking engines. The signal box closed in May 1987, the sidings which retained broad gauge sleepers have gone and the whole area is now heavily overgrown. The quarry too has gone - it is now a hill! Some may recall the article by local enthusiast Peter Gray, referring to these sidings also being used by the Torbryan Treacle Mines traffic. This was published on 1 April but still aroused much local controversy! HST power cars 43140 + 43145 are sharing the 10.50 Paddington - Penzance 27 May 1986

In the days before our rail network was decimated, Newton Abbot and Totnes were the two adjoining stations furthest apart on this route at just over eight miles distant.

TOTNES for ASHBURTON

Class 45 Peak has a respectable ten coach train - a long walk to the Buffet for those at the back! The station still had an interesting array of buildings and a GW pattern Mogo van in the bay. The footbridge was lost after being hit by a rail crane, requiring a replacement shuttle bus until it could be replaced!

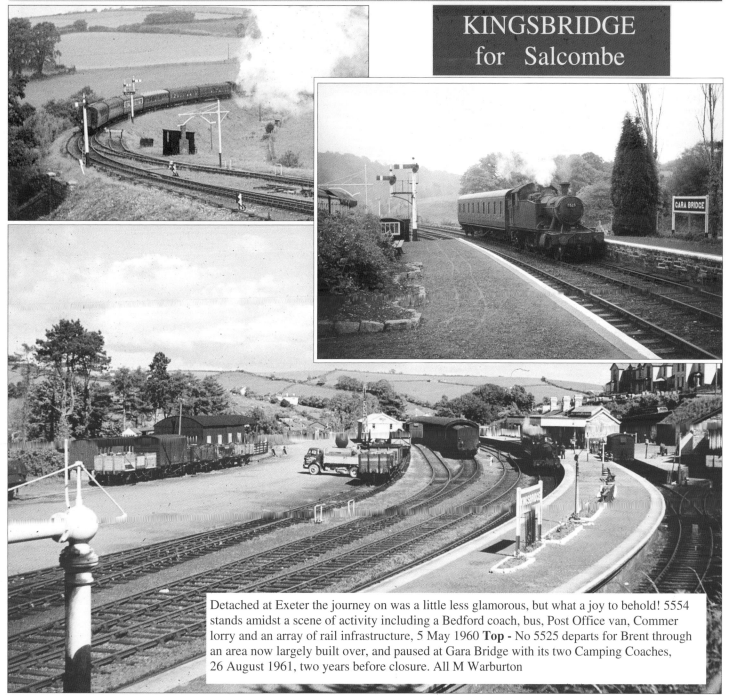

KINGSBRIDGE
for   Salcombe

Detached at Exeter the journey on was a little less glamorous, but what a joy to behold! 5554 stands amidst a scene of activity including a Bedford coach, bus, Post Office van, Commer lorry and an array of rail infrastructure, 5 May 1960 **Top -** No 5525 departs for Brent through an area now largely built over, and paused at Gara Bridge with its two Camping Coaches, 26 August 1961, two years before closure. All M Warburton

LODDISWELL

Right - The tragedy of the loss of the Kingsbridge branch has meant that the South Hams is still suffering from its isolation, although Salcombe remains a town of predominately second homes. Here, a couple of years after closure is a rather overgrown Loddiswell.
R Holcombe

Below - Junction for the branch was Brent with through workings continuing to the end of regular service in September 1963. The station lasted another year, the signalbox until December 1973. It has survived as a PW store but is set for imminent demolition. This will only leave the former Goods Shed, now a dental surgery.

Opening day at Ivybridge, 5 July 1994. Passenger numbers have increased slightly, but never to the extent that is needed to encourage the push towards other much needed reopenings. Perhaps, this could be down to its isolated location on the edge of town, at the top of a hill.

IVYBRIDGE PARKWAY

WINGFIELD VILLAS HALT

DEVONPORT (ALBERT ROAD)

DOCKYARD HALT

FORD PLATFORM

KEYHAM

ST BUDEAUX (FERRY ROAD)

Left + insets - Milepost 239¾ marks the Hemerdon Up distant with a Grange hauled local, topping the climb from Plymouth in the mid 1950s. The lead vehicle has the distinctive outline of a Hawkesworth coach. Clearly somebody is enjoying the warmth of a summers day, in the era before hi-vis clothing, but what is he doing, possibly a lampman?

Below - Another Grange (closer examination suggests 6822 or 6872, neither of which were then west country engines), on Laira embankment. At this time the tidal creek and boatyards on the landward side had not been covered by a dual carriageway. Low tide exposes the de-masted hulk of the *Antelope* built in 1906 at Brixham (still visible today). Across the River Plym is the woods of Saltram. Both c1958.

Plymouth can boast one of the earliest railway systems in this country having been built in the 1750s to facilitate the movement of stone blocks for the building of Smeaton's lighthouse, now rebuilt on the Hoe. The construction of the Breakwater was undertaken using ships equipped to carry truckloads of stone - surely what must be one of the first roll on / roll off train ferries!

Having had the remains of a once busy Taunton roundhouse on page 36, here is a corner of Laira - 'the lair of Kings', plus other more humble types of motive power. Left to right around the turntable are 5532 (now preserved), 7916 *Mobberley Hall,* 4920 *Dumbleton Hall* (now preserved) and 5544. At the demise of Laira as a steam shed, the last to engine to depart was 1363 the former Millbay Dock shunter. When called to go for scrapping, she developed a fault which could not be fixed until her preservation had been secured. In 1947 at the end of the GWR, Laira had an allocation of over 100 engines. Of the other sheds featured so far, Old Oak Common had 232, Westbury 71, Taunton 55 and Exeter 34.
D Luscombe coll A Crump

Travel from Paddington to Plymouth could be fraught, Agatha Christie used it for her murder mysteries *'4.50 from Paddington'* and *'The Plymouth Express'* (the latter a rather unlikely journey from Paddington via Bristol!).

The shed closed to steam at the end of April 1964, by which time the new diesel depot had taken over. Looking back towards the woods of Saltram, an Up train is disappearing off towards Tavistock Junction. To the left of it and in front of the houses, had been sidings used for stabling the Saltash auto trailers and also Laira Halt. The vacant space between the Mk 1 stock had once been the coal stage - the photographer standing on the site of the roundhouse with the Class 52 Western and stock where there had been an additional straight road shed dating from 1931.   M Boddy

The Great Exhibition of 1851 was immensely popular and many excursion trains would have been run from all corners of the country. One was reported by the *Western Times* starting from Plymouth and with several stops en route, by the time it left Bridgwater consisted of three engines drawing 52 coaches with 2,800 passengers! The contractors were to run another, two weeks later calling at all stations Plymouth to Wellington - epic journeys worthy of reporting!

After the GWR had bought their way out of the need to stop all trains at Swindon for a regulatory ten minute refreshment stop, the first through run from Paddington to the West via Bristol was the Cornish express, achieved by the introduction of water troughs at Goring. Departure time for this prestigious train was 10.30 am. As a result of a naming competition in the *Railway Magazine* for April 1904, the winning choices were combined to become *The Cornish Riviera Express* - but known to railwaymen ever since as *The Limited*.

The first non stop run to Plymouth was the Royal Train conveying the Prince & Princess of Wales to Falmouth on 14 July 1903. Hauled by 3433 *City of Bath* but having to run via Bristol even so this set the precedent for the *Cornish Riviera Express*.

PADDINGTON & PLYMOUTH

Kings were not allowed West of Keyham, due to their high axle loading. Hence the first stop for *The Limited* in steam days was at Plymouth where an engine change took place. Warship class D820 *Grenville* is most appropriate motive power, given the local association of Sir Richard Grenville (a name shared with the last of the GW Tenders working at nearby Millbay Docks) and the Devonport Dockyard of which there would soon be a grandstand view as the train passed high above at Keyham. Remodelling of the station was completed in 1962, by which time the newly completed regional offices were of little benefit as most of the SR 'withered arm' was soon to disappear.

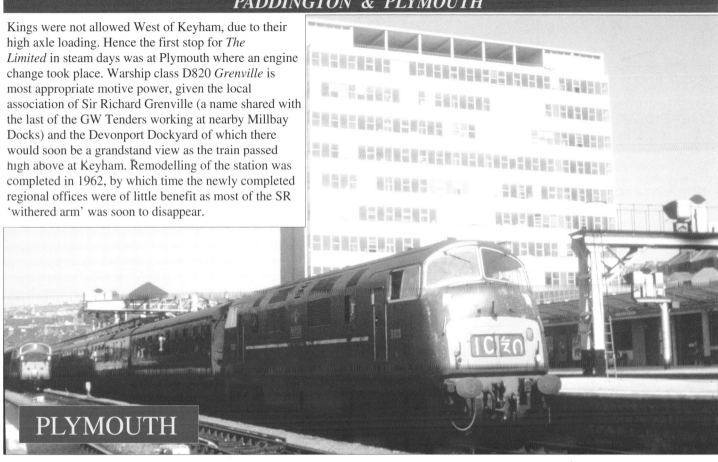

PLYMOUTH

SALTASH — DEFIANCE PLATFORM — ST GERMANS — MENHENIOT — LISKEARD — DOUBLEBOIS

Royal Albert Bridge Signal Box looks out over the Tamar while a Grange rumbles over the top of the SR line to Tavistock which passes under here. Note the foot crossing and single line token pick-up post, the ATC ramp nearby gave a repeat of the adjacent signal. This atmospheric scene was captured during the bridge centenary celebrations on 2 May 1959. M Warburton

The first officially confirmed time a King class loco crossed the bridge was on 9 May 1998 when 6024 *King Edward 1* entered the Duchy with a railtour from Coventry to Par, which it took over at Bristol. (There have been a number of earlier but unconfirmed claims of Kings being sent to Cornwall overnight during the Plymouth Blitz.)

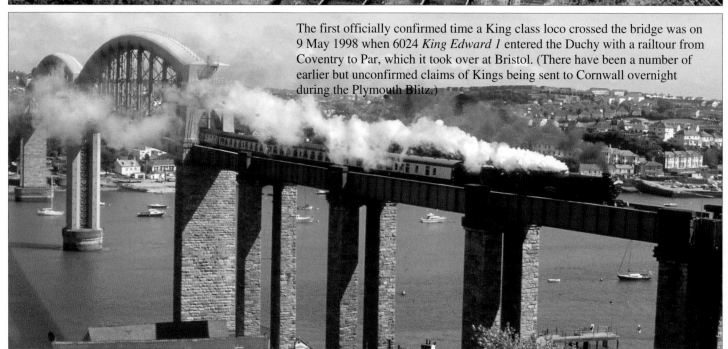

Brunel's masterpiece the Royal Albert Bridge. The two main spans, each 455 feet long and weighing 1100 tons were made on the Devon shore in front of the row of cottages on the far bank in this picture. Tens of thousands watched in silence as the first span was floated into place with pontoons under each end. It then took nearly a year to jack this up to its final resting place. In spite of the Navy insisting on 100 feet of clearance for their ships to pass under, the bridge was hit by *HMS Roberts* taking about ten feet off its mast, when the vessel was being taken upstream for storage c1950. Ten years later, the Up Cornishman has been captured for posterity on a cold February day. M Warburton

Road traffic had to wait another century for a bridge, from which the shots of 6024 and this one of 6988 *Swithland Hall* were taken. For much of the life of the railway bridge, the end inscriptions have been partially hidden by ladders and platforms (these have now been removed as access to the inside of the tubes is no longer permitted) which led to doors in to the tubes and over the top. A handrail along the top was provided for the benefit of Firewatchers in WW2, prior to which, there was only a four inch high toe rail for staff engaged in painting and inspection - clearly a good head for heights and strong boots were needed!

When opened at a cost of £225000, it had been possible to buy tickets to walk across the deck of the bridge, in the tracks of Prince Albert.

To commemorate its 150th Anniversary, Network Rail allowed this memorable walk to be repeated, an opportunity your author and many others were pleased attend.

No 6420 is running in sandwich formation with two pairs of trailers for an RCTS Special on 2 May 1959. One of several tours run in connection with the centenary celebrations which were also marked with a special poster by Terence Cuneo, a copy of which is on the station. (With sufficient enlargement, Cuneo's trademark mouse is to be found running across the track.) M Warburton

BODMIN ROAD   RESPRYN   LOSTWITHIEL   PAR For NEWQUAY   ST BLAZEY   LUXULYAN

Right - How the mighty are fallen, shorn of its canopy, the building has been badly neglected and fenced off. That was in August 2004, since when there is no sign of any positive progress, only further decay with the listed building now being regarded as at serious risk. Thankfully, work has been done to improve what is left of the rest of the station. The former goods yard has been built over. P Triggs coll A Crump

Below - The old bridge is dwarfed by the towers of the newer road suspension bridge. Taken from a passing train heading for Saltash, the PW lookout (with armband) and his men stand back from their work. The line behind them is the remaining stub of the original coastal route to St Germans.

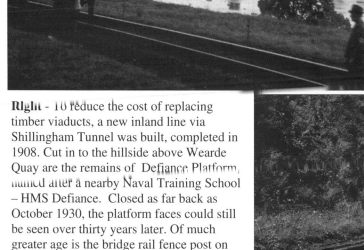

Right - To reduce the cost of replacing timber viaducts, a new inland line via Shillingham Tunnel was built, completed in 1908. Cut in to the hillside above Wearde Quay are the remains of Defiance Platform, named after a nearby Naval Training School – HMS Defiance. Closed as far back as October 1930, the platform faces could still be seen over thirty years later. Of much greater age is the bridge rail fence post on the right which dates back to the broad gauge era. D810 *Cockade* is heading the 9.25 Derby -Penzance. J Crowley coll A Crump

SALTASH to ST GERMANS

Left - Near Wivelscombe on the drive to Ince Castle the old trackbed has become overgrown and waterlogged. Occasionally the gardens are open to the public which enabled this view to be taken. Still lined with soot of mostly Victorian engines, this is an undeveloped corner of Cornwall-well off the beaten track. Ince Castle gave its name to Castle class loco 7034.

Below – D1048 *Western Lady* will hardly be taxed by a three coach train - but will she win the race along the platform? Just off the end of the platform had been the signal box and running downhill past the houses, was the course of a narrow gauge line to a quay on the River Tiddy, over which the main line timber viaduct was reputedly whitewashed to placate a neighbouring landowner. Opposite the loco was the yard closed in 1965, nowadays the location is perhaps better known for its range of vintage camping coaches. May 1976. D Homer coll A Crump

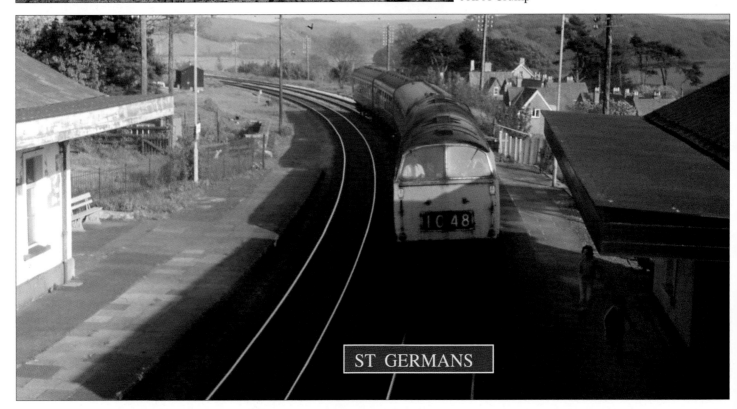

ST GERMANS

MENHENIOT

MENHENIOT

LISKEARD
CHANGE FOR LOOE

Above – 1960s Menheniot with its Brunelian bungalow style building - note how the platform has been widened to improve alignment of the curve through the station, using space gained by the abolition of the broad gauge in 1892. Only the Up shelter now remains. M Warburton

Left – On the station end of Liskeard viaduct is the last of the Cornwall Railway viaduct number plates *15* measured from their terminus at Millbay. The now lifted sidings were the site of an engine shed where in Victorian times one loco worked an early train to Millbay before spending the day shunting the docks and then working an evening train back again.

BUGLE • ROCHE • ST COLUMB ROAD • QUINTRELL DOWNS PLATFORM • NEWQUAY • ST AUSTELL •

Left - On a quiet Sunday afternoon in August 1959, the sound of 6934 *Beachamwell Hall* almost at the top of the 1 in 60 bank up to Liskeard would have carried far. 6934 was allocated to Wolverhampton Oxley at this time and so is surprising motive power for the St Erth - London milk train, perhaps she was on loan for the then busy summer holiday traffic. Just beyond the train, huts either side of the line mark the TPO mail apparatus site. Goods traffic is clearly still buoyant and served by three ex GW Thorneycroft Nippy delivery lorries. The distant skyline is of Bodmin Moor, and further right, Caradon Hill -where quarries created the need for a canal, and later a railway to Looe, for shipment of the product of the mines and quarries.
A Morris coll A Crump

Right - Less than seven years later in June 1966 and the town has grown considerably although freight traffic has ceased and the yard is used by Engineers and a raft of clay 'hoods' - for traffic from Moorswater. More recently this area has been cleared and the Up platform extended back to opposite the yellow gradient post.
M Warburton

COOMBE

Left - Descending the bank from Liskeard a 4575 series tank will pull up at Coombe while another of the same class which has worked up from Looe and run round, will return to Liskeard. Our train engine will itself then run round and set off for Looe - Coombe Junction was a busy place at the height of summer! 150 feet above the old route to Caradon, is Moorswater viaduct.

DOUBLEBOIS

The lifted platform edgings tell their own story of closure from 5 October 1964, but what a glorious setting to sit and watch the world go by! 17 June 1966.
M Warburton

The summit of the Cornish main line is just west of Doublebois, Then it is downhill past Bodmin Road to Lostwithiel. Through the Glynn valley is a succession of lofty viaducts, of which this is the curving 130' high Largin with a Castle hauled train made up of mixed ex GW stock in 1961. The slide that this is taken from was found in an American collection of holiday snaps!

THE BODMIN EXPRESS

Evidently overcrowded holiday trains are nothing new.

BODMIN ROAD
CHANGE FOR
BODMIN, WADEBRIDGE
AND PADSTOW

BURNGULLOW — GRAMPOUND ROAD — PROBUS & LADOCK PLATFORM — TRURO FOR FALMOUTH — PERRANWELL — PENRYN

Left + below – No 50 050 runs past the Unigate Creamery (closed 1991) at Lostwithiel, rusty rails and a solitary milk tank suggest that the long era of milk traffic by rail is drawing to a close. D1041 *Western Prince* rolls in with the 07.00 Bradford, both on 21 February 1976. B this time passenger services to Fowey had long gone, like the narrow gauge line that ran through the middle of this ancient capital of Cornwall and on under the main line to serve a nearby wharf in what is now Coulson Park with iron ore Also gone, are the Cornwall Railway buildings and even the clay sidings have not seen traffic for several years. The town was also home to the Cornwall Rly workshops, now converted in to flats. M Warburton

Left - Screaming Maybachs as a pair of Westerns make an impressive exit from Bodmin Road on the 14.00 from Penzance. *Westerns* D1056 +1053 *Sultan + Patriarch* leave their mark on the environment 21 February 1976. Services to Bodmin General ceased from 30 January 1967 hence the platform road has gone, but clay from Wenford lasted until 1983. Originally, this area had been served by a short lived station at Respryn, a little further west, still an access point and marked by the nearby 'Station Lodge'.   M Warburton

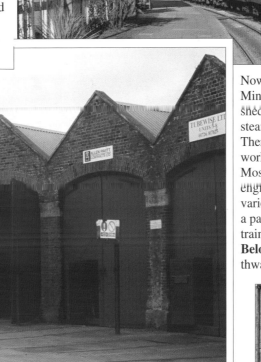

Now in industrial use is the Cornwall Minerals Railway semi-roundhouse shed at St Blazey which had closed to steam in 1962.and completely in 1987. There were nine roads in the shed, plus workshops and an S & T depot here. Most of the loco allocation was tank engines-many of them for use on the various china clay branches, along with a pair of heavy freight tanks for clay trains to Fowey via Pinnock Tunnel. **Below** – A familiar sign intended to thwart spotters in days gone by.

Right - Par Loop connects the main line to the Cornwall Minerals Rly Newquay – Fowey and Par Harbour branches. The CMR station for Par was renamed when the loop was opened, becoming St Blazey and closed finally in the mid 1930s having only been served by workmen's trains for the last decade. This is the old CMR station and later GWR signal box. **Below –** On the outskirts of St Blazey is Middleway Bridge Crossing - now devoid of its charming hut. Between the crossing box and the railway all the operating wires and rodding were carried on a bridge over a stream. On this side of the railway is what is left of the old canal that predated the railway. Operation of this and St Blazey Bridge crossing is now from the main signal box. Both March 1976.
 M Boddy

MIDDLEWAY BRIDGE CROSSING
GROUND FRAME

BR QUINTRELL DOWNS PLATFORM

Left - An unusual place, the waiting hut looks as though it should have the more common pagoda style roof. As can also be seen, the ground frame has been moved in to this end of the hut which carries the name-board *QUINTRELL DOWN SIDING EAST GROUND FRAME*, the siding having been taken out of use in 1965, six years before this picture.
M Boddy

Below left – A Swindon built DMU is passing the derelict trackbed of the line to Perranporth and Chacewater, at the triangular Tolcarn Junction in 1971. Services to Chacewater ended in February 1963 with much of the junction area now built over.

Newquay station has been, for most of its life, an important terminus. Carriage sidings on the left had extended across the car park to where a Western class diesel sits at the platform formerly used by Perranporth-Chacewater-Truro trains. Just above the DMU exhaust is the rather modest canopy and station offices. Built as a mineral line to the harbour, traffic there dwindled as passengers increased, finally the extension through the town closed in the 1920s. It went from near the black house, along what is now a footpath and down through a tunnel-now an aquarium. August 1972.   M Warburton

NEWQUAY

PAR change for NEWQUAY

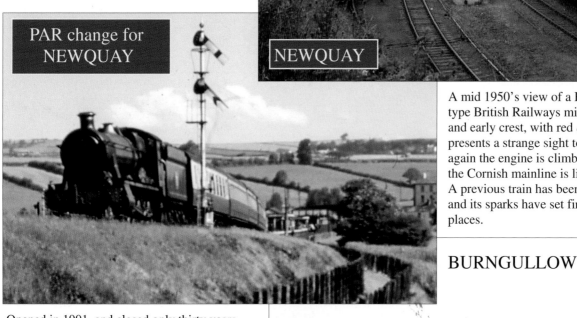

A mid 1950's view of a Hall class loco in the first type British Railways mixed traffic black livery and early crest, with red & cream livery coaches it presents a strange sight to GW enthusiasts. Once again the engine is climbing hard as it leaves Par - the Cornish mainline is like a roller coaster!
A previous train has been worked a bit too hard and its sparks have set fire to the grass in several places.

BURNGULLOW

Opened in 1901, and closed only thirty years later, the Up side waiting shelter lasted over a century – it was in the 'V' of the junction where the branch had gone to St Dennis but is now cut back to Parkandillack. On the other side of the branch was a small loco shed, and perhaps the better known reminder of the station was the signal box which lasted until 1986 when the line here was singled - it has since been doubled again in 2004. Also now out of use, is the vast modern, rail served complex of Blackpool Dries just before the station, a clear sign of the changing fortunes of the Cornish clay industry.

Clearly demonstrating the complexities of the history of the GWR main line from Paddington to Penzance, and how it is made up of a number of lines of independent origin. Falmouth had been an important port but lost much of that importance to Southampton because of its easier connection to London - by rail. To try and regain that prestige, Falmouth pushed for its own rail link. Too many years of infighting meant that the original aim was never fully achieved - but the Cornwall Railway from Millbay had its destination at Falmouth - the line seen running straight ahead here. The West Cornwall Railway had built their line east from Redruth to Truro terminating initially here as Truro Road and later at Newham. These two lines crossed here at Penwithers Junction (actually in Penweathers). Trains to Truro were diverted to the new station at Highertown and Newham became a freight only depot. An unused chord to provide a direct link between Highertown and Newham can be seen on the lower left. Branch freights continued to have to reverse and one can be seen waiting to cross and reverse, after the freight hauled by a pair of NBL D63's has passed. July 1960.
M Warburton

To FALMOUTH

To PENZANCE

Penwithers Junction Truro

Across much of Cornwall, the topography is such that viaducts abound. Brunel devised a system of timber fans, mostly on stone piers to try and keep construction costs down. Over time these needed replacement, some as at Largin on p89 had their piers extended and a new steel superstructure. Others like this one at Collegewood on the Falmouth branch had an entirely new replacement built alongside - a considerably easier operation, completed here in 1934. The timber viaducts were built from a number of standard sized components which could be replaced without too much difficulty, by skilled teams of men using little more than rope and a plank to work off, Worn out timbers were recycled into smaller sizes and eventually used to make furniture - recycling is nothing new! M Warburton

PADDINGTON & FALMOUTH

Only ever a single track branch with provision for doubling at tunnels and bridges, Falmouth was still a place of some importance with a sizable station area, almost all of which is now out of rail use. By the summer of 1977 the terminus was reduced to a single line dead end, the sidings to the left being for the adjacent shipyard. An overgrown wasteland to the right is where the main platform and Brunelian 'chalet' style station had been, all of this was cleared away in the late 1960s. Behind the photographer, a considerable wooden goods shed, yard and engine facilities have also gone. The still interesting journey now attracts more passengers than it has for many years.

FALMOUTH

DOLCOATH HALT · CAMBORNE · GWINEAR ROAD · ANGARRACK · COPPERHOUSE HALT · HAYLE

On the waterfront and close to Truro city centre, Newham station had a wooden overall roof rather like the well known ones at Ashburton or Moretonhampstead. Photographs here are rare and it is unfortunate that the old station - in the centre of this view - is hidden by wagons. Loco 5541 had been on the Cambrian section for many years, only spending a few months in the Duchy before transferring to Plymouth Laira to see out her days with British Railways. Withdrawn in 1962, she was later rescued from Barry scrapyard and can still be seen today. Shunting of this yard was interesting as there was no run round facility for the engines and instead gravity shunting was relied upon, using a headshunt near the gasworks. **Inset -** Newham is now covered by roads and industrial units, this branch closed 7 November 1971. From Gasworks Hill where an old bridge abutment provides evidence of where the line was, towards Penwithers is now a footpath, 15 July 1960.   M Warburton

Truro Newham

Evening draws in as our journey nears its destination. with an immaculate County heading West towards Chacewater and Scorrier being reflected in its train - at least the third coach is still ex GW in this late 1950s view over Penwithers Viaduct.

Along with other intermediate stations, Scorrier was closed, from 5 October 1964 and now only the platform remains mark the spot from a passing train. Beneath the station a tunnel carries a footpath on what was the trackbed of the Portreath Tramroad from Poldice Mine to Portreath Harbour. This historic line gave us what is now the earliest surviving rail passenger vehicle which rests in the Royal Cornwall Museum at Truro.

SCORRIER

Drump Lane Redruth

Redruth station has always been a very cramped and awkward site, being between a tunnel and a viaduct. When sidings were in use in what is now the car park, the adjacent viaduct of Carn Brea granite was built to include a headshunt over part of its length - a very unusual and expensive addition. Traffic, particularly coal, was also handled at West Yard off West End (now redeveloped as Gweal Pawl and a car park) which had been the West Cornwall Rly terminus before their extension to Truro. Increasing traffic required more space and a new depot was built off Drump Lane in 1912. Photographed in March 1976, traffic has greatly diminished, at least some of the wagons are for Engineers use. It has since been completely cleared and is currently a lorry park.
M Warburton

On the Redruth & Chasewater Railway (sic) opened in 1825, which ran from Redruth to Devoran - never reaching Chacewater, their Rule Book stated that to stop a train it was acceptable to violently wave a hat or any other object. Prior to the introduction of locomotives there were a number of passing loops on the single line, but if trains met in mid section lots were drawn to decide precedence!

At Carn Brea there is little sign of railway activity now, both the station and West Cornwall Railway works have disappeared. Camborne is still open - in every sense - given the lack of weather protection, but Holmans adjacent, famous engineering works is now housing. In the midst of further diversions from earlier routes (Camborne-Penponds and Angarrack-Hayle Wharf), lay Gwinear Road station. **Below –** Other destinations were available but never rail connected-these were another reminder of the extensive GWR road motor operations in West Cornwall. On a wet August day in 1961, 4563 is arriving from Helston and the Signalman is ready to take the single line staff. M Warburton **Inset –** The lengthy crossing gates were the first in Cornwall to be replaced by barriers - this station has been swept away apart from the rubble remains of the platforms. M Boddy

GWINEAR ROAD
for HELSTON
THE LIZARD, MULLION
and PORTHLEVEN

ST IVES SECTION ST ERTH LELANT CARBIS BAY ST IVES MARAZION PENZANCE

HAYLE WHARF

Above - Several of the sidings around Hayle Wharf were not able to be worked by locomotives and so horse power continued. July 1960. M Warburton

Inset - The North Crofty branch was between Camborne and Carn Brea. P Mitchelmore

Right - The very unusual signalbox and behind it the branch dropping away, most of the sidings having been lifted. M Boddy

5,000—W 20—6-15.   (999-1)
GREAT WESTERN RAILWAY.
HAYLE WHARVES to
NORTH CROFTY BRANCH.

Date _____ 191 . Wagon No. _____

Consignee _____

HAYLE

ST ERTH for
ST IVES

4570

CARBIS BAY

CAFÉ

SHOP

Above - That most vital element of any Great Western branch line scene a 45xx and B Set, in this case 4570 - another long time Penzance engine which moved to Plymouth for the last few months work after West Cornwall was dieselised. The lower level bay platform at St Erth is still used by St Ives trains inspite of the best efforts of Dr Beeching. Off picture to the right was the now closed dairy, that site and the yard are planned to become car parking for a new Park & Ride such is the level of usage at Lelant. July 1960

M Warburton

Left - Later the same day, a return working from St Ives was captured as it wound its way around the cliffs-surely one of the most beautiful views to be had from a train window anywhere.

M Warburton

ST IVES

Childhood memories of the beach at St Ives and its golden sands at a time when the station served rail passengers, rather than the motorists and their cars as parking space. Too late it was realised that cars would swamp and spoil the town. **Right -** No 4564 has just arrived on a very busy 24 August 1961, with coaches everywhere-including two Camping Coaches by the goods shed. No 4564 was the last incumbent of St Ives shed which was to close only a couple of weeks later on 9 September. High above the town the ex railway owned Tregenna Castle Hotel, commands a fine view over the picturesque old town and its harbour.   M Warburton

TREGENNA CASTLE HOTEL

ST IVES ENGINE SHED

Another of the October 1964 closures was Marazion, with freight following fifteen months later. Historically this was a more important place than Penzance, in more recent times it was noted for its produce traffic. To take advantage of the superb views across Mounts Bay to Newlyn and St Michaels Mount, three ex SR Pullman cars were installed here in 1962 with another three added from Fowey when that line closed in 1965. Twenty years later the coaches were out of use and having only been used by the BR Staff Association, they were suffering from their close proximity to the sea and attracting attention from as many vandals as enthusiasts. Two were moved to Petworth station in Sussex as part of a hotel, the remaining hulks were apparently burnt out by c2006 and the cleared site has now been redeveloped. The six cars had been *Calais, Flora, Mimosa, Alicante, Juno, Aurora* (thought to be in that order Left to Right), with *Mimosa* and *Flora* going to Petworth. Dating from 1912 *Alicante* was the oldest, vehicle present whilst *Calais was* one of the earlier twelve wheel cars.

MARAZION

Penzance site soon became too crowded to cope with engine servicing which moved out to Long Rock in 1914- but retained the GWR code *PZ.* for its modest twenty five engines . Beyond D1027 *Western Lancer* is the redundant coaling stage with its 45000 gallon water tank, to the right of which is the four road shed, repair shop and boiler house. Steam had been withdrawn on September 10 1962. Diesel loco usage continued to 1976, the depot site was cleared 1976-7 and new facilities built to cater for HST's. Taken in June 1975, the imprint of the Up main can still be seen in the ballast, the line here having been singled in 1974. M Warburton

PENZANCE

July 1960 sees Hawkesworth pannier 9433 with shunters truck bringing in empty stock, the surf is up and holidays beckon …..M Warburton

The end of the line comes with posters for milk, Mackeson and Guiness, along with a choice of taxi's! *Through the Window* gave a rather more romanticised view of Penzance, hidden coves with sunny beaches, and the increasingly wild landscape out to Lands End and The Lizard, needless to say, the area was well served by the pioneering GWR roadmoters too!